GOVERNMENT BEYOND THE CENTRE

SERIES EDITOR: GERRY STOKER

The world of sub-central government and administration – including local authorities, quasi-governmental bodies and the agencies of public-private partnerships – has seen massive changes in recent years and is at the heart of the current restructuring of government in the United Kingdom and other Western democracies.

The intention of the *Government Beyond the Centre* series is to bring the study of this often-neglected world into the mainstream of social science research, applying the spotlight of critical analysis to what has traditionally been the preserve of institutional public administration approaches.

Its focus is on the agenda of change currently being faced by sub-central government, the economic, political and ideological forces that underlie it, and the structures of power and influence that are emerging. Its objective is to provide up-to-date and informative accounts of the new forms of government, management and administration that are emerging.

The series will be of interest to students and practitioners of politics, public and social administration, and all those interested in the reshaping of the governmental institutions which have a daily and major impact on our lives.

GOVERNMENT BEYOND THE CENTRE

SERIES EDITOR: GERRY STOKER

Published

Richard Batley and Gerry Stoker (eds)
Local Government in Europe

Clive Gray
Government Beyond the Centre

John Gyford
Citizens, Consumers and Councils

Richard Kerley
Managing in Local Government

Steve Leach, John Stewart and Kieron Walsh
The Changing Organisation and Management of Local Government

Arthur Midwinter
Local Government in Scotland

Yvonne Rydin
The British Planning System

John Stewart and Gerry Stoker (eds)
Local Government in the 1990s

David Wilson and Chris Game (with Steve Leach and Gerry Stoker)
Local Government in the United Kingdom

Series Standing Order

If you would like to receive future titles in this series as they are published, you can make use of our standing order facility. To place a standing order please contact your bookseller or, in case of difficulty, write to us at the address below with your name and address and the name of the series. Please state with which title you wish to begin your standing order. (If you live outside the UK we may not have the rights for your area, in which case we will forward your order to the publisher concerned.)

Standing Order Service, Macmillan Distribution Ltd, Houndmills, Basingstoke, Hampshire, RG21 2XS, England

Local Government in Scotland

Reform or Decline?

Arthur Midwinter

MACMILLAN

First published 1995 by
MACMILLAN PRESS LTD
Houndmills, Basingstoke, Hampshire RG21 2XS
and London
Companies and representatives
throughout the world

ISBN 0-333-63765-8 hardcover
ISBN 0-333-63766-6 paperback

A catalogue record for this book is available
from the British Library.

10   9   8   7   6   5   4   3   2   1
04   03   02   01   00   99   98   97   96   95

Copy-edited and typeset by Povey-Edmondson
Okehampton and Rochdale, England

Printed in Malaysia

For my wife Jean
a truly generous spirit

The research for this book was supported by a grant from Lothian Regional Council

Contents

List of Tables   ix

List of Figures   x

*Foreword by Councillor Eric Milligan, Convener, Lothian
Regional Council*   xi

Preface and Acknowledgements   xiv

1   The Political Context   **1**

2   The Road to Reform   **11**

   History   11
   The classical model   13
   Local government in the polity   18
   The Thatcherite challenge   23
   In search of a new consensus?   28

3   Reforming Local Government Finance   **30**

   The politics of local spending   30
   The new council tax   34
   The grant and capping system   36
   The new financial orthodoxy   39
   Developing VFM in Scotland   44
   Problems of methodology   45
   The implications for practice   51
   Conclusion   53

4   Privatising Municipal Provision   **54**

   Public choice analysis   54
   Extending competition   58
   Promoting choice   64
   Constraints and contradictions of privatisation   78

5   Reshaping Local Authorities   **86**

The government's arguments   86
The research evidence   88
The arguments reviewed   94
The costs of reform   99
The illusion of accountability   105

6   Defending Local Government in Practice and Theory   **110**

Beyond the radical rhetoric   110
The politics of opposition   115
The case for municipal provision   120
The case for the Wheatley system   132
The erosion of local democracy   136

7   Problems of Implementation   **142**

Introduction   142
The problem of Scotland's water   142
The problem of transferring services   147
The problem of controlling costs   152
Conclusion   156

References   158

Index   168

List of Tables

2.1 Functions of local government in post-1929 system 12
3.1 Comparison of local budgets and government assessments in Scotland 38
3.2 Type of Performance Indicator (PI) 49
4.1 Ratio of municipal/'private'/voluntary premises in residential care 69
5.1 Current allocation of local government services in Scotland 90
5.2 Satisfaction with local services 91
5.3 Electoral competition in local government 93
5.4 Range of population size of optional authorities 97
5.5 Predicted costs/savings of reform 101
5.6 Spending on key services in Scottish Regions/Islands 1992–3 104
6.1 Budgeted manpower in Scottish local authorities 121
6.2 Income from fees and charges 122

List of Figures

3.1 Performance review in context   48
3.2 Selected performance indicators (PIs)   49
3.3 Measures of performance   50

Foreword

Councillor Eric Milligan, Convener,
Lothian Regional Council

In 210 BC, the Roman historian Petronius observed of his experience of the Roman Army:

> we trained hard . . . but every time we were beginning to form up into teams we would be reorganised. I was to learn later in life that we tend to meet any new situation by reorganising; and a wonderful method it can be for creating the illusion of progress while producing confusion, inefficiency, and demoralisation.

The recent history of local government has been exactly analogous to this. At the time of the reorganisation of local government in 1975, there existed a broad consensus that change was required. A widespread and genuine enthusiasm for the proposed restructuring into regions and districts was apparent, and the new system was imbued with the confidence that many of the emerging problems of urban and rural development could be addressed successfully by means of the powers and responsibilities of the new local councils.

Unfortunately, these hopes and aspirations have been substantially dulled by extensive and continual intervention by central government. The obsessive determination to control and constrain the public sector which grew in the early 1980s has been justified on the basis of the control of public spending, and the perceived need to make our public organisations more accountable. The style and approach which has been adopted by central government in its declared intention of achieving these ends, however, has had the direct effect of reducing the effectiveness of the public sector bodies subjected to this treatment, and undermining belief and confidence in the public sector as a whole, and local government in particular. I fear that it may be some considerable time before that confidence is restored.

The successful operation of the current system of local government, therefore, has been achieved despite the attentions of central government, and is largely attributable to the inherent qualities of the post-1975 system, and the abilities and commitment of the people who made it work.

It is easy to forget how fragmented and disparate local government was before the 1975 reorganisation took place. These problems manifested themselves in a lack of direction, effectiveness and ambition amongst the local councils. We can be proud now of the consistent and uniform standards of local services which exist across the country. The regional councils in particular can be seen to have contributed to the undoubtedly high quality of life which the huge majority of the Scottish people now enjoy. And for those people who live in conditions of hardship and in vulnerable circumstances, through the commitment and innovation of local authorities such as Strathclyde Regional Council, the very maximum of local discretionary powers has been used to support and protect the most needy and vulnerable in society.

Scotland's regional councils have also brought a vision and breadth of perception to the physical development of our country. The bringing together of economic, land-use, and transportation needs within a coherent strategic framework, which is so essential to the future prosperity of Scotland, has been achieved in a way which has reconciled the apparently irreconcilable, and ensured a consensus amongst a wide range of public, private and voluntary interests.

The direct benefits of these efforts can be seen across Scotland, and in particular in West Lothian, where an effective partnership involving Lothian Regional Council, the local district council, Lothian and Edinburgh Enterprise Limited, and private business interests, has revived and revitalised a declining local economy. The grim prospect of continuing decline in the mining and heavy industries has been replaced by the influx into West Lothian of companies at the very cutting edge of new technologies.

All of this helps to ensure that Scotland and the regions of Scotland can take a respected and authoritative place amongst other regions in Europe. The credibility of Scotland's regional councils, working individually or in partnership with others, has been instrumental in winning the financial support from Europe which is essential to local economic development.

In my years in local government as an elected councillor, and when I was privileged to serve as President of COSLA and as Vice President of the International Union of Local Authorities, I have been witness to an enormous variety of local government systems and approaches across the world. I have also had the opportunity to see at first hand attempts to introduce new systems of local government into areas or attempts to reform existing systems. In the light of that experience, I cannot see the current attempts to reorganise local government in Britain as anything other than a determination to further undermine the capabilities and autonomy of locally accountable government.

The desire to uproot the existing system and recast it according to the tenets of a political philosophy is not a result of grassroots dissatisfaction. Rather, the push for reform has come exclusively from central government, and it must be seen in the same context as other politically driven initiatives such as compulsory competitive tendering, the growing use of quangos in the management and provision of public services, and increasing control by central government. Its effect will be to reduce the effectiveness of local councils, prejudice the continuation of demonstrably successful partnerships, and diminish the standing of local government in Britain and in Europe.

The future of local government will be more secure, the better it is generally understood. For this reason, I have been very pleased to assist Arthur Midwinter in his research on which this book is based. Professor Midwinter's national and international reputation is firmly based on his detailed knowledge of local authorities, and his publications have promoted a broad understanding of the role and operation of local government. I hope that this book will influence and inform policy-makers and all who have an involvement or interest in this most vital part of the governance of this country.

Preface and Acknowledgements

This book is concerned with recent changes and reform proposals in the structure, finance and scope of local government. The Conservative strategy seeks to promote economic efficiency and consumer choice. My concern as a student of democratic politics is that the downside of these changes is a diminution of organisational efficiency and political choice. Hence the sub-title 'reform or decline?'.

So this book is both a policy critique of recent reforms, and a personal statement about the role and scope of local government. My views have been formed on the bases of twenty years involvement with local government, as researcher, analyst and consultant. Although I am critical of key aspects of government policy, I am also clear that what is on offer is progress compared with the Thatcher decade. Finance is a good example of this progress. And though I am pessimistic that structural reform will bring little economic and social benefit, I am also confident that the reforms will not have the disastrous impact that the poll tax did in the late 1980s. Rather, my objection is that the reforms tackle unreal problems, and a little serious consideration and critical policy analysis would have avoided unnecessary reforms.

The potential for a book such as this emerged during the preparation of research papers for Lothian Regional Council. Eric Milligan quickly offered to support this initiative. Eric has a rare combination of political talent and good humour, and consistently encouraged me to complete the work timeously. Tom Aitchison, David Hume and other Lothian staff assisted generously with access to information to assist the research. Marian Keogh and her staff at the Scottish Local Government Information Unit did likewise, and Marian offered helpful comments on the first draft. Conversations with Grant Jordan and Murray McVicar, who were also studying reform, stimulated my thinking on the issue.

In my own office, Jean McDougall, handled the secretarial context of the research with her customary efficiency, and Neil McGarvey proved an invaluable reference-chaser and discussant of the key issues.

As ever, the support of my family eased the process of production. My wife Jean has never shared my infatuation with things political, but has always encouraged my endeavours nevertheless. This book is dedicated to her with gratitude.

ARTHUR MIDWINTER

'The new single-tier, all-purpose authorities will be better able to promote effectively the interests of the area they represent. They will be able to identify more with their area. They will be more accountable to the people who live there. In sum, they will reflect the diversity of Scotland as a whole and *revive the dynamism of local democracy*.'

(Scottish Office, 1993, p. 36)

1 The Political Context

In 1990, the Conservative government announced its intention to reform local government into a system of unitary authorities. It also intended to ring further changes to local government's role in service delivery through the extension of competitive tendering, and a further restructuring of its financing.

Local government has faced a consistent stream of reforms since 1979. It has been portrayed in political rhetoric as bureaucratic, inefficient, and unresponsive. In the local press, the occasional bureaucratic error or politically sensitive decision receives widespread coverage. The routine of local government – the steady and consistent delivery of public services, achieved with a high degree of political consensus – goes unrecorded. Rather, the focus is on anecdotal illustrations of bureaucratic incompetence or in the petty insults and point-scoring which regrettably often passes for debate in local government. Good news is no news.

This book is an attempt to redress the balance. Scholarly works by their very nature do not receive the media coverage of bureaucratic errors or political conflict. Nevertheless, a reasoned case for the local government system remains a worthwhile intellectual exercise. Despite the imbalance in treatment, the Scottish public continue to have greater faith in local than central government, and high levels of satisfaction with a broad range of local government services. For too long, this consensus has not been reflected in public policy.

The Conservative government's approach to local government is at best a negative and distrustful one. Its proposed structural reforms should be seen as part of a wider strategy of reconstructing the role and scope of local government, with greater reliance on market provision.

This book, therefore, is a work of *political argument*. It states the case against the government's philosophy, and defends the classical model of local government, that of municipal service provision with a degree of local democracy. It argues that critiques of municipal bureaucracies are wanting, and fail to square with the high level of satisfaction with municipal services; and it argues that a political

1

strategy of fundamental change is unlikely to succeed, whereas incremental change in a system of consensus politics is more likely to promote lasting change. In short, the right's claims that major savings, greater efficiency and responsiveness will be delivered from reform are a gross exaggeration: the rhetoric of reform falls short of the reality of practice.

The book is also a work of *policy analysis*. It examines the assumptions and arguments underpinning the government reforms against the existing research evidence, and assesses their potential impact in the light of our understanding of how the system actually works. It shows that most of the claims made for reform are unfounded: rather than delivering a more local, more efficient and more accountable local government system, the combined effect of the government's package of reforms is a shift from local to central accountability at no clear fiscal benefit, and a fragmentation of local responsibility.

It is necessary, however, to place the government's reform strategy into the Scottish political and administrative context. Within the union, Scotland has enjoyed a distinctive system of administrative devolution, with its own system of law, education, and local government. It has a Secretary of State who serves in the Cabinet. Thus:

the Scottish Office is an acknowledgement of the territorial dimension of administrative responsibilities. This dimension finds reflection in the policy autonomy enjoyed in some fields and the scope for
policy experimentation afforded in others by the distinctive legal and
local government inheritance.   (Judge, 1993, p. 7).

Much of this devolution was developed by Conservative governments. Mitchell (1990) sees two reasons for it – appeasing nationalism and promoting administrative efficiency. This process, however, is used to reinforce Scotland's distinctive position in the British 'union state':

the union state is not the result of straightforward dynastic conquest.
Incorporation of at least parts of its territory has been achieved
through personal dynastic union, for example by treaty, marriage or
inheritance. Integration is less than perfect. While administrative
standardization prevails over most of the territory, the consequent
political union entail the survival in some areas of pre-union rights
and institutional infrastructures which preserve some degree of

regional autonomy and serve as agencies of indigenous élite recruitment. (Rokkan and Urwin, 1983, p. 11)

The existence of distinctive civil institutions, administrative devolution and a strong sense of national identity, however, should not lead to confusion about the place of Scotland in British government: its decision-making powers have been limited by government policy and Cabinet responsibility. Scottish ministers have a strong lobbying role *within* the British system, but policy consistency rather than autonomy has been the norm. Thus:

> Our survey of Scottish government has indicated that the scope for Scottish innovation is small, tightly constrained by the demands of Cabinet and party government and the unitary state. Yet Scottish demands are increasingly differentiated from those of England. This is placing the mechanisms for managing Scotland within the unitary political system under great strain. (Midwinter *et al.*, 1991, p. 202)

This was particularly so during the 1980s. The Thatcher government, elected on a programme of radical change, sought deliberately to dismantle the Keynesian consensus of the post-war era. Public spending cuts, privatisation and greater efficiency in government were key elements of its drive to reduce the role of the state. During this decade, the Conservative vote went into consistent decline. Between 1945 and 1960, deviations in voting patterns north and south of the border were few, but the Thatcher years saw a trend to regional patterns of voting behaviour:

> The Englishing of the modern Conservative Party has clearly played a part. Since 1979, the Tory benches in the House of Commons have been significantly more 'southern' than before . . . In all, less than 10 per cent of Conservative MPs elected in 1979 and 1983 came from Scottish and Welsh seats, and only 16 per cent from the north of England (the smallest proportion for over one hundred years). (McCrone, 1993, p. 173)

For some on the political right, the explanation for the Conservative decline in Scotland was the failure to apply full-blooded Thatcherism. Scots were portrayed as prime examples of a dependency culture, and the Scottish Office budget as a 'slush fund' (Midwinter *et al.*, 1991).

In practice, however, Scotland was not exempt from the strategy. All the key elements – privatisation, public spending cuts, council house sales, the internal market reforms in the NHS – can be found in Scotland. In a review of the issue, Holliday (1993) observes that in the 1979–87 period, Thatcherism was mainly macro-economic in focus. Only in 1987–90 did Thatcherite radicalism enter the realms of major reform of the welfare state, in education, health, housing and social work. Resistance came not from political institutions, but from the Scottish public. Therefore, it is more realistic to argue that the Conservative decline in the 1980s was more the result of the application of Thatcherism than not. The disaffection Scots felt for the Conservative government was significant: after ten years of Thatcher governments, 78 per cent of Scots felt there should be no more privatisation, 85 per cent felt that subsidising employment was justifiable, 74 per cent said they would oppose the privatisation of the health service, and 74 per cent opposed the poll tax. By contrast, greater public support was found for more managerialist reforms.

Thatcherism, then, became recognised as one of the causes of Conservative decline in Scotland. In practice, the Thatcher style, strident and confident, implied greater ideological content than in fact materialised, with the real exception of the privatisation of the nationalised industries. Where Thatcher differed with traditional Conservatives was fundamentally over the role of the state.

Ian Gilmour's impressive interpretation of the nature of Conservatism is a useful one for comparison with the Thatcher agenda. Gilmour believes that the post-war consensus was more of a Tory consensus than a Labour one, reflecting the latter party's revisionism after thirteen years in opposition. His view of the Conservative political stance since 1945 can be summarised as: 'general welcome of the welfare state; full employment; the encouragement of ownership of property; the acceptance of trade unions; the mixed economy; support for private enterprise; and strong defence' (Gilmour, 1978, p. 19). Margaret Thatcher's agenda accepted only half of these. The collection of ideas known as the 'New Right' is a combination of classical economic liberalism, and classical conservatism, with its belief in a limited but authoritative state. In addition, it includes the new economic theories of monetarism and public choice. Ideologically it prefers conviction politics to consensus politics; a minimal state to the welfare state; and markets before political resource allocation.

This is indeed a substantive difference of philosophy. Traditionally Conservatism rejected abstract political and economic theory, and favoured pragmatism and experienced judgement in the tackling of governmental problems, an approach which brought some electoral success to the party in the middle of this century. As McCrone notes, however: 'this version of Toryism laid stress on civic duty and social responsibility rather than on reductionist individualism. If anything, the political ideology of neo-liberal Thatcherism moved away from its social and ideological base in Scotland rather than vice-versa' (McCrone, 1993, p. 138).

Whereas the conventional ideology made much of catering for Scottish political distinctiveness, the Thatcherite strategy of reducing the State directly challenged much of the Scottish political consensus, and the emphasis on accommodation and pragmatism which was central to traditional territorial management (Bulpitt, 1983). Thus:

> Scotland has not been exempt from the key elements of the strategy, for the simple reason that the conventions of British government would not allow it. The British political programme was applied, with the Scottish Office refraining from independent policy initiatives, and concentrating on a conventional defence of Scottish interests within the framework of that programme. (Midwinter *et al.*, 1991, p. 208)

The political consequence of the Thatcherite electoral success – albeit with a historically low share of the vote for a governing party – was to resurrect in the late 1980s the campaign for constitutional reform. Much of the running on this issue was made by local government itself, spurred on by the erosion of its own powers under Thatcherite policy. The Convention of Scottish Local Authorities (COSLA) amended its constitution to allow it to address the wider issues of Scotland's governance, and to provide administrative support for the cross-party Constitutional Convention, which included MPs; MEPs; church representatives; local authorities; trades unionists; business; women and ethnic groups. Its strategy was to

> seek challenging and fundamental reform of the structure of government in the United Kingdom. A Scottish Parliament securely based on legislative power will give responsive and direct government to

the Scottish people whilst retaining essential links with the rest of the country. It will put an end to the unacceptable situation in which policies radically affecting education, housing or health can be imposed by Ministers out of touch with Scottish opinion.   (Scottish Constitutional Convention, 1990, p. 7)

Disaffection with policy, combined with Labour's weak position electorally in UK terms, was interpreted as requiring fundamental constitutional reform. Those who had opposed devolution in the 1970s for the most part fell silent in the face of the seeming invincibility of Thatcherism in England. Increasingly, the question of the Conservatives' lack of a mandate in Scotland, and Scotland's democratic deficit in receiving policies it did not want and vote for, were raised in the political agenda by the Opposition. Historically, Labour has 'accepted the legitimacy of Conservative governments lacking majority parliamentary support in Scotland and Wales because the practice of alternation in government would, in due course, allow them to govern without a majority in England' (Jones and Keating, 1988).

The disintegration of consensus politics polarised politics ideologically and territorially. In terms of the British Constitution, this is not a problem: Westminster governments rule throughout the UK. But as the Prime Minister himself recognised, that Union can only survive through consent, and that 'cannot be assured by giving people in other parts of the Kingdom things they do not want' (Major, 1992, p. 11). The 'no-mandate' argument is in practice an argument for self-determination. The Conservatives' lack of a majority of votes or Scottish MPs has resulted in the marginalisation of Conservatism in Scotland. Yet, ironically, the achievement of constitutional change is now wholly dependent on Labour's performance in England, and such a revival would recreate the conditions for alternating governments and reduce the political need – in policy terms – for constitutional change.

This is not the place for an extensive consideration of the proposals for constitutional change. It remains the case that these are still best regarded as a political response to the electoral threat of Scottish nationalism by an essentially Unionist party. It is certainly the case that disaffection with Thatcherism in Scotland created stress in the political system. In the long term, however, 'there was little evidence up to 1983 of the Tory south of England, despite its population, imposing its political will on the Celtic periphery' (McCrone, 1993, p. 150); and as

Punnett observed, 'the supposedly dominant south of England has been on the winning side less often than has Scotland' (1985, p. 28).

The solution of a Scottish parliament is by no means as obvious as some observers assume. Holliday's otherwise sound analysis of the limits of Thatcherism concludes that:

> whereas Thatcherism had little difficulty in out-smarting many of Scotland's formal political institutions, it found a major challenge when confronted by Scottish culture and Scottish public opinion. This battle it clearly lost. Indeed, over the course of its 11 years in power, Thatcherism presided over, and in many respects provoked, similar decline in Scottish support for the British State.
>
> This familiar manifestation of informal limits to Thatcherism is highly likely in the 1990s to generate fundamental restructuring of the Scottish political order, a prospect which remains anathema to militant Thatcherism. A new Scottish political settlement will be the final indication that Scottish public opinion, which mounted substantial resistance to Thatcherism, rightly regards existing political structures as incapable of placing effective limits on alien political radicalism. (Holliday, 1993, p. 409)

This conclusion needs modification. First, it is also the case that support for the fully blown Thatcherite agenda is a minority view in England. As Crewe (1989) has clearly shown, Thatcher won elections, not hearts and minds. It is often forgotten that the poll tax – held up as an alien imposition in Scotland – was opposed fiercely in England and played a crucial role in Mrs Thatcher's defeat. Despite the Scottish public's dislike of such policies, they would prefer to see them changed rather than seek political reform, which remains a low priority amongst Scottish electors. The tepid support for constitutional reform is a reflection of wider political and economic discontent with governmental performance: this does not require structural change, but policy change.

This is exactly the approach adopted by the government. They decided to defend the Union in the 1992 General Election, and were attacked – in my view wrongly – for polarising the issue. This stout defence of the Union, in a context where the national question was given considerable prominence in the political debate, resulted in a modest recovery in the Conservative vote. The Prime Minister himself made a keynote speech in Glasgow in defence of the Union:

For we do not do it for party political advantage. It is not the
Conservative Party that gains – or has gained –most from the ties
between Scotland and England. And yet it is a party that supports
the Union. Not because it has always seemed good to us, but because
it has always seemed right to us.   (Major, 1992, p. 8)

The Major years marked a distancing of the government from
Thatcherism. John Major's approach is founded on

a commonsense view of life from a tolerant perspective. He is
pragmatic but with a pragmatism confidently based on underlying
principles. By looking at issues on their merits, John Major is
actually taking the radical agenda further than his predecessor did.
At the same time, he is far more in the mainstream of tradition than
his critics.   (Lang, 1994, p. 4)

Major's approach was to acknowledge the Thatcherite inheritance but
reclaim traditional Toryism. In the Scottish context, ministers publicly
admitted past insensitivity to Scots. The Scottish Secretary called for

a new tone and new mood in Scottish politics. In doing so, I was
seeking to strike a note of reconciliation where before there had been
confrontation. We have sought to adopt a less ideological and more
pragmatic and commonsense approach to the business of government'.   (Lang, 1992, p. 7)

A more consultative, consensual style was then on offer, supported
later by a commitment to greater policy autonomy to meet Scottish
needs from the Scottish Office. The essence of the change of style was
summed up thus by Lord Fraser:

We must seek, where possible, to frame policies which are not only
good for Scotland, but which are acceptable to most Scots. The
introduction of the Community Charge in Scotland a year earlier
than anywhere else in Britain, while done for the best of motives, was
widely resented and alienated many Scots. It would be unwise to run
the risk of creating such resentment again, for ultimately it would be
the Union which would pay the price in terms of loss of sympathy
and support.   (Fraser, 1992, p. 7)

Subtle shifts in emphasis followed. Scottish spending, which had been
attacked in 1990, was defended in 1992 as being a benefit of the Union.

The retention of a formula-based approach to public spending would erode Scotland's historic expenditure levels only very slowly (Heald, 1994). Convictions and ideology were relegated in importance. Lang's perspective is clear enough:

> An ideology is often the rationalising patina that is overlaid, in hindsight across a range of decisions and events that at the time were much less certain in their outcome and much more pragmatic in their development. And anyway, Conservatism is, by tradition, instinctively undogmatic. Undiluted ideology simply produces two-dimensional politics, when everything is seen in right angles. That critical third dimension of the context in which decisions are taken is ignored. Ideology can become a substitute for thought and an ideologically-driven party ultimately becomes a pastiche of itself, entirely in the grip of ideologues applying uncritically yesterday's answers to to-day's problems. (Lang, 1994, p. 3)

This change in emphasis is an incremental one. Government policy, and inherited commitments, cannot be radically altered overnight. Most of the 'managerial' agenda of the 1980s, in the form of competitive tendering, decentralisation, choice and efficiency remained central to Conservative strategy, although wholesale dismantling of the welfare state was out.

The Conservative government of the 1990s, however, remains faced with hostile local authorities. The Conservatives' own power bases have been dramatically reduced – they do not control any regional council, and only a handful of small districts. They are still faced with philosophical opposition to their own vision of local government, and with a public waiting to be convinced of the merits of their approach. This is a context they have recognised and are seeking to influence, but Scotland will undoubtedly remain infertile soil for Conservatism, although the promise of a more conventional Conservatism was welcomed by the Scottish press:

> The tone of Mr Lang's address suggests he is embarked upon a path more promising starting from the Scottish Tories than that achieved in the bad old Thatcherite days. If Mr Lang is as good as his word and reduces the ideological content of his programme while raising the pragmatic approach, there may be yet much to applaud.
> (*Scotsman*, 8 October, 1992)

The Conservatives have recognised the differing ethos in Scottish politics and society and since 1992 the government has been seeking to create a political climate more in tune with the Scottish psyche, which could assist policy implementation and – of course – its own political future. A few regained seats in Scotland could be crucial in the next General Election.

Yet the commitment to reform the structure, role and financing of local government predated the development of 'taking stock' – and like any reform, still requires to be grounded in realistic assumptions and accurate diagnosis to be successful. In the remainder of this book, I shall evaluate the reshaping of local government in the 1990s. Despite the government's view that it was reforming with the benefit of multi-party support for a single-tier solution, the boundaries of that system would also reflect their own singular view of the changing role of local government. To this end, their approach remains one of reform without consensus.

2 The Road to Reform

History

The history of local government in Scotland is a recent one. It was in the legislation of 1889 that the basis of a modern local government system was laid. Prior to that, Scotland was administered by a fragmented system of councils, boards and committees. The three basic units – county, burgh and parish – had widely different origins. Counties had been created for law enforcement purposes in the early Stuart period; burghs originated in the twelfth century, with powers of law enforcement and the regulation of trade; and parishes were units of church organisation, which provided some primary education and administered poor law relief. There were 33 county councils, 201 town councils and 869 parish councils. In addition, there were 33 commissioners of supply and 98 district committees, plus several standard joint committees, district boards of control, and distress committees (Martlew, 1988). In short, there was nothing resembling a system, nor local government as we know it today. Rather, there was fragmentation through separate provision of services, and a limited franchise, in a system of 'ratepayer democracy' with separate rates and grants to finance them (Midwinter, 1990).

The process of modernisation was a response to industrialisation, and urbanisation. In Scotland, municipal initiative in the nineteenth century led to the provision of water, gas, and hospital and public health services such as baths, wash-houses and laundries, to cope with the consequences of poverty and poor housing. In 1889, several ad- hoc boards were abolished and a new system of multi-purpose authorities controlled by democratic election was created. This also marks the growth of central interest in local government, in terms of passing mandatory duties on the new local authorities, and creating an administrative structure in Edinburgh for their supervision (Alexander, A., 1982a).

11

The parish schools had been replaced by a system of elected school boards which was rationalised to 37 education authorities in 1918, and then to the county and city councils in 1929. The 1929 reforms simply rationalised the existing structures, by eliminating the parish unit, transferring powers to larger units, and distinguishing between larger and small burghs. This eliminated the ad-hoc authorities, and left a complex system with four cities, 33 counties, 19 large burghs, 173 small burghs, and 198 district councils. The range of functions varied, and have been well summarised by Clive Martlew (see Table 2.1).

Table 2.1   *Functions of local government in post-1929 system*

Counties and cities	All functions
Large burghs	All functions except education and:
Small burghs	Valuation, housing, minor roads, street lighting, cleansing and refuse collection, sewerage, assistance to industry, regulation of shops, markets, and so on, burial and crematorium, places of entertainment, parks and recreation.
County councils	Outside burghs: all functions Within large burghs: education and valuation. Within small burghs: education, health, social work, valuation, police, fire, planning, classified roads, public health, registration, weights and measures.

Source: Martlew, *Local Democracy in Practice* (1988) p. 6.

This was not the end of the matter. The inappropriate population geography of several authorities led to *joint arrangements* over the provision of police, fire, water and sewerage, creating all-in-all a complex structure which was not conducive to clear accountability. Joint Boards in particular received opprobrium in submissions to the Wheatley Commission, which concluded:

> there is a hearty dislike of the system of requisitioning, on the grounds that it separates to an unacceptable degree the responsibility for spending money from the responsibility for raising it. These complaints are loudest from the burghs which have to pay – willy nilly – the County requisition, but they also arise in relation to requisitioning by joint committees.   (Wheatley, 1969, para. 82).

The classical model

The twentieth century saw local government lose some of its powers over health, gas and electricity, but receive considerable new powers in the fields of planning and social work, while the creation of the welfare state, with its emphasis on a comprehensive approach to public welfare, greatly expanded the volume and quality of provision in both community and personal services. Local government emerged as the major mechanism of service delivery in the modern welfare state: local authorities became, in Stoker's words, 'major spenders of public money and providers of public services' (1988, p. 3). They were intended, moreover, to be not just units of democratic expression, but also mechanisms for the dispersal of power in a pluralist political system.

> Salisbury's proposals for local government were based on a fear not of centralising monarchs but of the centralising tendencies of a popular franchise. In his view, the enfranchisement of the working class would make welfare politics the central electoral issue, and lead inexorably to the rise of a powerful administrative state. This would be avoided only by the creation of new local authorities whose value as counterweights would be realised 'by diminishing the excessive and exaggerated powers' of central government'. (Widdicombe, 1986, p. 48)

Although there has been no coherent theory of local government, it has reflected the political values of pluralism and accountability. There has been variation of service delivery and political management of local government, but the essential characteristics of local government have remained the same throughout this century, and can be summarised as follows:

- they are directly elected by popular franchise;
- they are multi-purpose;
- they have responsibility for service provision within a defined geographic area;
- they may only act within the specific powers set by Parliament;
- they have power to raise total taxation; and
- they are corporate bodies whose powers are vested in the whole council.

The organisation of local government reflects these characteristics and the reform process which converted separate authorities into multifunctional ones on a piecemeal basis. The main unit of service delivery is a local authority department, staffed and managed by professionals. These professionals are responsible to an executive committee of the council, and through it to the council as a whole. We shall call this the classical model of local government.

In the 1960s, there was discontent in the Scottish Office at the inappropriateness of the post-1929 structure of local government for modern society and economy. Planning and government intervention was in vogue, and a regional tier of government to facilitate capital investment in infrastructure was deemed necessary (Ross, 1980). A White Paper proposing the 'modernisation' of local government in Scotland through creating fewer larger authorities which would bring unity to urban areas with their rural hinterlands was allowed to lapse by the 1964 Labour government, but the ideas survived and influenced the Wheatley Commission which sat 1955–69. When it reported, it noted that local government structure remained as it had been in 1929, despite forty years of the greatest social change in our history. It urged that the evidence it received was convincing that many local areas had been shown to be inappropriate; that authorities tended to be too small for the functions they had to discharge; that the relationship between different kinds of authority was over-complicated and made for conflict rather than harmony; and that the relationship of local with central government did not promote a proper sense of local responsibility.

Much of the Wheatley analysis was concerned to improve efficiency and democracy in local government: larger authorities would provide economies of scale and more efficient use of resources, and would permit the provision of specialist services, while at the same time eliminating the need for joint arrangements and close central government supervision. It saw the twin purposes of efficient service delivery and democratic choice as the 'raison d'etre' of local government. Although there were alternative modes of provision, Wheatley could see no viable alternative which could administer the whole range of local services satisfactorily while retaining the principles of democracy.

Its basic objective, therefore, was a fundamental shift in the value of power between central and local government. Strong and vigorous local government would permit effective government to be brought close to the people (that is, from the centre). Reorganisation was a way of removing the obstacles to effectiveness, and rationalisation of the structure would permit greater coherence, better value for money, local sensitivity, and a strengthening of local democracy. In the light of the emphasis on joint arrangements for small authorities in the current agenda for reform, it is worth quoting Wheatley at length. Local government was needed to 'sustain a viable system of local democracy', but 'local' did not necessarily mean small scale:

> Local democracy has been construed in the evidence as embracing local consciousness, historical continuity, 'grass roots' government and 'the smallest practicable unit of administration'. Witnesses have been led into such strange assertions as that the removal of financial responsibility contributes to local democracy; that financial viability should inevitably be secondary in importance to the need for local democracy; and that local democracy is promoted by such practices as requisitioning and indirect election.   (p. 48)

Wheatley interpreted local democratic control as part of a wider system of democracy – 'to act as a catalyst of local action and reverse the growing power of Whitehall' (p. 48).

The rationalisation of the structure and the elimination of joint boards would lead to a more direct form of control and accountability, as large authorities would be important power blocs in a pluralist political system. This is a theme we shall return to, but the argument was well summarised in the report itself.

> Traditional concepts of local democracy can result in very small units, but only with a corresponding sacrifice in standards of performance. Local democracy, thought through, does not involve this sacrifice at all. On the contrary, it is when local government operates at the scale which its services demand that true local democracy emerges: because that is the point where power and responsibility can be properly entrusted and where the administration of services can become responsive in the right way, that is through pressures from within rather than from without.   (p. 50)

Wheatley's proposals reflected its view of efficiency and democracy – it concluded that the areas of local government no longer accorded with patterns of life and work; that authorities were too small to administer their responsibility effectively and efficiently; and that many authorities were heavily dependent upon central government grant for their income. The result was that the balance of power and responsibility between central and local government had gone wrong, with a movement of power towards the centre, and greater interference in administrative matters.

To overcome this, Wheatley recommended the creation of seven new regional authorities, with responsibility for *strategic services*, the major local government functions of police, fire, water and sewerage, roads and transport, education, social work, housing and planning; and 37 district councils responsible for *environmental and amenity services* of a local nature. Recommendations were also made for a system of community councils with consultative powers to act as a voice for local communities.

Wheatley therefore proposed the creation of a new unit of local government based on economic geography – the region. It was bigger in concept than metropolitan government, as it stretched beyond the city suburbs into its rural hinterland. In its purest form, a region would have an administrative and commercial centre – usually a city – to which the inhabitants of an area would travel for business, shopping and recreation (for example, Edinburgh in Lothian, Inverness in the Highlands). The regional concept was difficult to apply fully in areas such as the rural Borders or industrial Fife. The parliamentary process led to a modification but not rejection of the proposals, with some changes to regional and district boundaries. The plan to divide Fife around Dundee in the north and Edinburgh in the south failed, and a Fife Region was created. Borders Region was carved out of the Lothian administrative unit, and the three islands areas of Orkney, Shetland and Western Islands from the Highland Region.

The system did not have the easiest of baptisms, and a populist critique emerged – focusing around the concept of size, and arguing that the new authorities were too big, bureaucratic, and remote. These are elusive concepts to analyse, and have seldom been used with any precision in political debate. Uncertainty over the future of the system was reinforced by the 1970s debates on political devolution. For example, a Scottish National Party policy document argued that local government reform was a mistake. It talked of 'monster regions' and the end of 'local' government, and advocated the abolition of all regional councils and the transfer of their powers to existing districts, with strategic services being transferred to a Scottish level of government. The Liberal position is similar, although it sees the need for *fewer* districts. The Labour Party dealt with the matter quite simply

– it argued that the structure of local government would be a matter for the new Scottish Assembly to decide. In 1977, a Conservative local government review group concluded against radical change, but recommended a review *within* the existing structure.

The proposals for local government reform which link it to constitutional reform should clearly be recognised as proposing the 'loss' of local powers, by centralisation to an assembly or greater use of joint boards. The solution is not nearly so simple and straightforward as its advocates assume. The Conservative government elected in 1979 did appoint a Committee of Inquiry, which became a minor tidying-up exercise concentrating on concurrent services. Districts assumed responsibility for leisure and recreation, tourism, countryside planning, nature conservation, war memorials and caravan sites. The major recommendation that regions should assume sole responsibility for industrial development was rejected by the government. Responsibility for the major services remained the same, and the representations of the four cities and of Argyll and Bute and Moray districts were rejected (Stodart, 1981). In the case of the islands councils, the Montgomery Inquiry (Montgomery, 1983) reported a good bill of health and no significant changes were made.

Conflicts between regions and districts have arisen, partly over concern at loss of status in the cities. Alan Alexander (1982b) concludes that 'the overall impression is of a system that functions because the goodwill and informal networks of members and officers act as lubricants for a structure in which friction is inherent' (p. 134). Alexander's judgement, however, is based on the anecdotal perceptions of participants rather than an analysis of the policy and service delivery consequences of this 'friction' – he simply points to the officers who regard liaison committees as 'useless'. Perhaps there is less reason for the committees than a simple focus on structure would suggest, but no clear and convincing study of the 'problems' of region district relations exists.

Finally, the argument has often been made that the new structure is more costly than its predecessor. Page and Midwinter (1981) examined this issue in some detail. They found a substantial increase in expenditure following reorganisation, but concluded that this was not attributable to reorganisation itself. Growth in capital expenditure in 1972–73 increased revenue expenditure after reorganisation. Secondly, revenue expenditure rose *before* and after reorganisation, in line with government policy, and the growth for 1975–76 was *lower* than the two previous years. Spending then actually *fell* in 1977–78. The higher rates of 1975 resulted from a combination of inflation, grant reductions, and increased spending on services. Although for some citizens, rates bills rose as they were incorporated into larger units with higher spending, this was not a feature of the system as a whole. This study concluded that the 'sweeping statements about their remoteness, inefficiency and cost are not generally supported by the available evidence' (p. 461).

Whatever the arguments about structure, there was a widespread consensus within Scottish local government on the fundamentals of organisation. The classical model is still commonplace, with:

● local service provision directly by a professional department of the authority, funded by a budget;
● executive supervision of its functioning by a committee of the council;
● council priorities determined through political debate in the full council chamber; and
● democratic control exercised by citizens through the electoral process.

It was this particular model and the assumptions underpinning it which became increasingly questioned by Conservatives, and radical reform reached the political agenda in the 1980s.

Local government in the polity

So far, we have considered reforms to the *system* of local government as a mechanism of service delivery. It is also an instrument of political choice, and thus a focus of normative arguments as well as political analysis.

In its early years, local government was looked upon as a valuable bulwark against the central state (Sharpe, 1970). This view of local government has come under challenge. In his book *Urban Political Analysis*, Patrick Dunleavy (1979) argued that the dominant picture of local government as electorally responsive, effectively representative, or indeed locally orientated in any democratic sense, is misplaced or unfounded. Local politics is seen as fundamentally epiphenomenal or surface activity which does not determine in any effective way public policy decisions. This is indeed contrary to the norms of British representative government, where the notion that election to public office is a prerequisite of effective and responsive government is deeply embedded. In local government terms, there is little in the way of a priori theory about the principles of local government (Hill, 1974). Rather, there are certain conditions and values. These include the rights of citizens to participate, whether as candidates or electors, equality of rights and treatment, and the rights of local communities to differ in terms of service and taxation levels.

Within the tradition, there has been continuity of four fundamental principles:

- *The* ultra vires *principles* – local government is a creature of Parliament and may act only within the specific powers set by it.
- *The local discretion principle* – local government has more than mere administrative discretion and can vary its use of statutory powers on the basis of local choice.
- *The taxation principle* – local government has a right to levy a prescribed form of local taxation.
- *The representative principle* – local government has statutory powers vested in the council as a corporate whole, whose membership is determined by direct election.

Together, these characteristics provide for a distinctive role for local government in the British political system. It is the single elected political institution apart from the House of Commons, giving it a political legitimacy that appointed boards and agencies do not have.

The essence of democratic local government is that it should meet the aspirations, needs and wants of its citizens. This is not to argue that it will do so perfectly, for just as markets do not respond perfectly to consumer demands, neither does the political system. It is argued, however, that local government has become particularly unresponsive because of the nationalisation of local politics. Local elections have been described as a 'sort of annual General Election' (Newton, 1976), and Miller (1988) has summarised neatly the implications for the notion of responsible democratic local government. With analysts assuming that the local election results reflect government popularity, attention focuses on the implications and consequences for central government rather than on the reasons for local results: local elections send messages to central government about its policies, not to local authorities about theirs.

That local elections do provide partial evidence of general shifts in support is clear enough. In part, this is a reflection of the level of analysis used by researchers, focusing on aggregate data results using regression analysis. Statistical analysis of this would not reveal the effect of party organisation and local policy issues. Using a case study approach, Bruce and Lee (1982) observed that the degree of uniformity in local election results is not high. Miller (1988) concluded similarly that both national trends and local variations occur. Even then, the argument remains that though national factors are dominant, local effects occur.

Midwinter and Mair (1987) argue that the problem is in part conceptual in terms of defining political issues as 'national'. Local government allows the expression of political values in the locality, and this in itself is an expression of local choice, rather than, as has been assumed, a reflection in spatial divisions over highly localised (that is, geographic) political issues. Voters use elections to express their political values, and a strong argument can be made that 'national trends' result in part from elasticity of definition and the research technique applied. Following the political polarisation and erosion of consensus of the 1980s there is increased evidence of local policy effects. Local elections can reflect both national swings (disaffection with the governing party) and local political choices. This view of electoral behaviour is consistent with the findings of studies of General Elections: voters are perceived to have broad perceptions rather than detailed knowledge of parties' philosophies and policies, and utilise a 'synoptic' evaluation of the issues, not detailed appraisal of manifestoes (Rose and McAllister, 1988; Heath *et al.*, 1985).

Once local government is considered as an important aspect of the national political system rather than as a self-contained democratic system in its own right, more realistic and relevant appraisal of its benefits becomes possible. In the Widdicombe Report (1986a,b) these are described as pluralism, participation and responsiveness. Local government is viewed as a mechanism for dispersing political power to communities, allowing for greater democratic influence over public policy, and promoting political participation by individuals. For pluralists, local government encourages participation, and has a capacity to learn, respond, change and win public loyalty. It permits local political choice (Jones and Stewart, 1983).

If we are to understand the nature of the political relationship between central and local government, then we must begin with a recognition that there is a high level of interdependence between them. Central and local government share the same electors, and hence popular pressure reinforces the conflicts and organisational tension which exists.

Central government's interest in local services is clear enough, whether through ensuring minimum standards are met, or simply requiring provision and leaving the definition of need to local authorities. The interdependence is reinforced through joint financing, and both central government's macroeconomic concerns over spending, and micro-political concern over specific tax levels. In the case of service provision, departments vary in their concerns and how they promote them, but overspending, political philosophy and strategy are important influences (Peacock and Wiseman, 1961). Recognition of the interdependence of the system has been accompanied by increased recognition of pluralism in the polity. Policy implementation has become difficult because of the 'number of dependency relationships' and 'acts of non- compliance' which arise in 'complex processes of interaction' (King, 1975).

Local government is not an autonomous entity. Its mould is shaped and constrained by the centre. It has a degree of autonomy, however, through which it responds to political preferences in the locality. Its constitutional basis is a limited one, but there has been a set of contentions over the years, for example, that local government has the freedom to fix its own spending and taxation levels, whereas the centre should be able to control borrowing for economic management reasons. In the 1980s, however, the political and fiscal context of local government underwent rapid and erratic change, with ministers asserting their constitutional superiority. Indeed, Scotland came to be regarded as the guinea-pig for local government reform, despite the initial caution shown by the Secretary of State (Midwinter, 1984).

The *structure* and *process* of central–local relations differ from England, and in part this is a reflection of relative size. With a population of around 5 million, only 65 local authorities, a single department of state and a single local authority association, less formal and more extensive consultation is the order of the day (Page, 1978). At the organisational level, this relationship is acted out in a series of joint committees between the Scottish Office and COSLA, although informal solving of problems is also a feature (Midwinter *et al.*, 1991, p. 149). Within the Scottish Office, however, there are spending departments and resource departments. The former often constitute alliances with the professional departments in the local authorities, in functional policy networks; and the latter are often linked in consultative relations in *expenditure* networks, where political difference can be important (Rhodes, 1987a).

Thus too much should not be made of the closer relations and simpler structure in Scotland. When one examines the *output* of the process – legislation, policy advice and resource frameworks – there is a remarkable congruity between Scotland and England (Carmichael, 1992). This includes, for example, common approaches to financial controls, fiscal systems, the role of public housing, community care in social work, and so on. In short, central–local relations in Scotland are distinctive for how decisions are made, rather than the substantive decisions themselves. Informality may overcome administrative problems, but it does not impinge on politically driven policy initiatives. The nature of the relationship is also similar. For most of this century, arguments about centralising trends have been common north and south of the border. This has arisen from a combination of the growing financial dependence of local government, and the extension of detailed administrative controls (Wheatley, 1969; Layfield, 1976). However, it must be clear that central control is a relative rather than an absolute concept: departments vary in their political objectives through regulation, direction and encouragement.

The empirical evidence on the impact of financial dependence on policy is not convincing. By contrast, there is evidence of considerable diversity of budgetary response (Midwinter, 1990). Similarly, though the scale of grant support infers dependence, the form of grant provision (that is, a block grant unhypothecated between services) confers discretion. Central government can use grant levels to influence total spending, while permitting diversity of response. A broad concern for service development still leaves local discretion over the scope and form of development. Central–local relations are characterised by bargaining and interdependence, and this is reflected in the outputs of the process. Local authorities can lobby through political and administrative channels, and have financial and informational resources at their disposal for bargaining. Although without doubt there are elements of hierarchy and control in the relationship, there are also mechanisms for local influence and degrees of policy discretion.

Relationships between central and local government are also complex, involving consultation, bargaining and decision-making.

Control in the absolute sense would be a heroic accomplishment by central government. The key issue is whether changes which reduce local discretion and enhance central control are a necessary and/or effective means of balancing national interests with local political choice. In official parlance, this relationship was termed a 'partnership', and prior to 1979, reflected the political consensus in power of a mixed economy with a large public section, in which local government was the main instrument of service provision in the locality. The election of a radical, reforming Conservative government challenged the basis of the consensus in the 1980s, converting the partners into adversaries, through the new government's more limited vision of the proper role of local government.

The Thatcherite challenge

The conventional model of local government has gone almost unchallenged for most of this century. Public services, professionally staffed and budget-financed, provided directly by the local authority under the executive control of a service committee – this is the established norm in local government. Private sector usage has been confined to specific aspects of provision, for pragmatic, localised reasons (Ascher, 1987).

When the Conservative Party came to power in 1979, it had a radical agenda to roll back the state, to reduce public spending, taxation and borrowing, and to make public services more efficient. But it had no clear set of policy instruments in mind at that time. Some elements in Conservative politics, known as the 'New Right' because of their broad adherence to the set of intellectual ideas of the same name (King, D. 1988), were vociferous advocates of reform, but they were not in a majority in the Conservative Party. Policy developed in an incremental way, on the basis of ideas *and* experience. The personification of these ideas in the term 'Thatcherism', and their embodiment in a particular style and tone of political argument, has spawned a whole series of academic works and competitive interpretations of the nature of the phenomenon (Kavanagh, 1987; Skidelsky, 1988). Some argue that the 1980s marked an abrupt, radical change to the course of British politics (Gamble, 1984); others that in practice the government did not provide the break with consensus it claimed for itself, as its performance seldom matched its rhetoric – public spending and taxation remained high, public provision remained the norm (Riddell, 1983).

The set of ideas which underpins Thatcherism lies in the realm of economics. Conservatives have always had a strong preference for the market sector over the state, even though Conservative governments presided over the growth of the latter. New Right economists, however, added to the conventional bias by arguing for *monetarism* – the need to control the money supply as the central instrument for containing inflation, and *public choice* – the economic analysis of government.

In evaluating the impact of Thatcherism on local government, it is necessary to examine the relationship between ideas and rhetoric; and policy and practice. In the local government context, the government's economic strategy and spending priorities require a reduction in local spending and taxation. It was not until late in the Thatcher years that public choice analysis, which regards public provision as inefficient and unresponsive, seriously influenced policy. Public choice analysis is a deductive form of reasoning from the central assumption of economics, that politicians, bureaucrats and electors act rationally in their own self-interest. Bureaucratic monopoly provision, financed by taxation, leads to 'oversupply' of public goods, because of the weakness of political control mechanisms. Bureaucrats pursuing budget- maximising strategies are 'supported' by the political process, not controlled by it, leading to budgetary growth, as programmes have constituencies of support in the form of highly organised interest groups. The result is:

> Sponsors are usually internally fragmented into committees or departments, which are staffed or backed up by politicians whose interests are closely convergent with those of the bureau, especially because they have an above-average demand for agency outputs. Bureaucrats best serve their own welfare by pushing continuously for budgetary growth, which increases their numbers, improves promotion prospects, allows the bureau to be more easily managed, creates areas of discretionary patronage or possibly perks fiddling, and generally builds up organisational slack and improves job security. Because agencies are so weakly controlled by sponsors, and because the budget-maximisation goal is open-ended, bureaucracies *inherently* oversupply outputs . . . (Dunleavy, 1986, p. 16)

The main works in the field are at the level of theoretical argument and lack empirical support. It must be concluded that the concept of 'oversupply' would be problematic for any researcher, as public provision seeks to *promote* consumption. However, in the hands of the political New Right in Britain, the arguments are regarded as confirmed, and thus public policy decisions can seek to overcome the vested interests of key groups (Pirie, 1992). From this perspective, professionals and their client groups are regarded as powerful vested interests distracting from economic performance. They become powerful groups to be curtailed.

Bureaucratic paternalism, unresponsiveness and inefficiency are all identified as undesirable consequences of traditional local government (Walker, 1983; Henney, 1984). This has led within the Thatcherite wing of the Conservative Party to an increasing questioning of the conventions of democratic politics in local government. The arrival of Nicholas Ridley as Secretary of State for the Environment resulted in a more upbeat approach to implementing municipal Thatcherism, as did the appointment of Michael Forsyth as Chairman of the Scottish Conservative Party. The New Right agenda for local government became mainstream in the late 1980s, and consisted of arguments for:

- greater reliance on *charging* for services;
- greater use of *competitive tendering*;
- greater use of independent evaluation of performance by *consultants* and *auditors*;
- the *fragmentation* of large local authorities into smaller units.

The New Right's argument is that competition and choice, and thus responsiveness to consumer preferences, will be enhanced by such changes: charging will reduce the oversupply which results from 'free' provision; competitive tendering will induce clearer policy specifications and better information about costs than conventional budgets; independent evaluation will be much more critical than self-evaluation; and smaller local authorities will be more socially homogeneous and thus more likely to reflect consumer preferences. This analysis has been challenged:

- bureaucrats and politicians 'care' about policies, not just their own self-interest (Goodin, 1982);
- not all bureaucrats seek to maximise budgets, and the result is not necessarily oversupply (Dunleavy, 1986);
- making policies based on simple economic maxims can be dangerous when the theory lacks empirical confirmation (Jackson, 1985);
- some bureaucrats will welcome contracting-out (Dunleavy, 1986);

- small local authorities and fragmented delivery systems can cause problems of co-ordination and duplication (Pollitt, 1986).

In short, the world of local government is more complex than the assumptions of the public choice theorists.

In Thatcherite rhetoric, however, local government was an object of outright contempt. One apologist describes it as Mrs Thatcher's 'biggest bugbear'. Extravagant spending programmes, trade union dominance, even 'quasi-revolutionary' activity have been portrayed as the norm in local government:

> The Thatcherite response was absolutely predictable: the govern-
> ment set out to achieve a 'paradigm shift' through the introduction
> of the privatization of local services; to increase the scope for
> individual choice (and hence encourage the virtuous virtues) by
> reducing local government's tax-based expenditure; and to make
> local government accountable to the local populace in the hope that
> this would restrain councillors from engaging in the promotion of
> their fancies at the expense of their ratepayers. (Letwyn, 1992,
> p. 177)

Local government policy was often presented in such polemical terms as an entire system characterised by extremism, profligacy and unaccountability (Newton and Karran, 1985), although such stridency does not normally elicit willing compliance from those being attacked. However, some writers share this vision of radical change: Moore (1991) has observed a fundamental restructuring of the local political economy, which challenged the established rules and conventions of central–local relations: 'non-ideological disputes, basic consensus, consultation and accommodation, and underlying this the legitimacy of local democracy' (p. 78). This restructuring, he believes, is a major source of turbulence to local authorities in maintaining a role as service providers and policy-makers.

The real test for the radical reconstruction thesis is not the emergence of ideology and hostile rhetoric in central–local relations, but policy impact – the existence of rhetoric should not of itself be construed as evidence of change. Bulpitt (1989) has argued that the Conservative government pursued a statecraft strategy towards local government in protection of its own interests, in which 'ideology will only be pulled in to justify, or add gloss to, behaviour and decisions already determined by statecraft considerations. Hence 'Thatcherism', in so far as it purports to be a serious political doctrine, is relegated to the back seat' (p. 56).

There were two central elements to the Thatcher government's approach to local government – a concern for economy (reductions in local expenditure) and a concern for efficiency. The first of these was part of the traditional Conservative scepticism about state activity, albeit reinforced with a monetarist dimension. The efficiency issue, however, had a more distinctive New Right thrust: where possible, government should be reduced and markets used to meet demands and where municipal provision is necessary, there is a need to ensure greater efficiency in the use of resources, through market surrogates.

In Scotland, some Conservatives have argued that the full rigours of Thatcherism were not employed (Fry, 1987). There was certainly a different 'tone' to central–local relations in the early years of power, but Scottish ministers too adopted a hostile approach to local government in the 1980s. The latest study of this question has been by Paul Carmichael, who asked if Scotland was different. He recognised that the Thatcherite 'approach' constituted a fundamental breach with consensus politics and the 'spirit' of central–local relations in Scotland, and noted the 'growing chorus of disquiet issuing from English Conservatives over public spending and the 'dependency' culture in Scotland. Conservative electoral decline is attributed by him to Scotland being denied the benefits of a rigorous application of full-blooded Thatcherite policies. In his comprehensive survey of local government policy in the Thatcher years, he points to the common experience of British local authorities in terms of:

- grant reductions;
- the introduction of compulsory competitive tendering (CCT);
- the sale of council housing;
- parental choice in education;
- capping controls on spending;
- the community charge (Carmichael, 1992).

In practice, however, New Right ideas only marginally influenced policy. Of those discussed above, only CCT and the Community Charge are strictly 'public choice'. The more radical parts of the New Right agenda have not been pursued: there was no great shift from public finance to user charges; no voucher system in education; no wholesale abandonment of planning; all of which were advocated by New Right think-tanks such as the Adam Smith Institute.

Municipal Thatcherism had a brief high watermark from 1987 to 1990, when the community charge was introduced and CCT expanded, new audit powers were introduced to limited effect and the provisions for opting out of schools for local government were announced. However, by 1990, New Right radicalism was in retreat. The community charge – the most developed application of public choice analysis – was a disaster and hastily abandoned. Mrs Thatcher's demise brought the promise of a more consultative, less abrasive approach to local government. Much of Conservative policy for the 1980s remained in place in terms of competition and choice, which was described as a fundamental transformation in municipal provision (Bailey, 1993). This would certainly be so in theory, but what of practice?

In search of a new consensus ?

After the 1992 General Election, the Scottish Secretary, Ian Lang, called for the change in the tone and mood of Scottish politics and a less partisan, less ideological approach was promised. A review of Scotland's government brought little change in terms of structure and factors, but promised a subtle and substantive change in the conventions of public policy, in the commitment to develop the role of the Scottish Office as an autonomous policy-making department in its own right (Scottish Office, 1993b). The document recognises that the strength of Scottish identity poses a challenge 'to respect and cherish the differences between each of the constituent parts of the United Kingdom'. This will be achieved through 'a distinctively Scottish approach to policy-making' which seeks 'Scottish solutions for Scottish problems' (p. 19).

This would also involve a return to a more consensual approach. A lengthy consultation process was promised over the reform of local government, and, moreover,

I see this reform exercise as one which will make local authorities more powerful and more effective organisations than at present, capable of commanding greater respect, and of exercising greater influence among the communities they serve. I regard the two-tier structure as an impediment to strong local government. I want to see established a network of dynamic new local councils, much stronger than either of the existing regional or district councils. Only then will we see the revival of local democracy which we all seek. (Lang, 1992, pp. 2 and 3).

The Secretary of State was offering a heady brew of strong, accountable local government. But such symbols are often appealed to by reformers to legitimise change. In the remainder of this book, we shall examine the range of fiscal, organisational and structural reforms introduced in the 1990s. Only by such a broad canvas can the real scale of change be properly understood.

Municipal Thatcherism did present a fundamental challenge to the conventional system of local government, but in practice it was a mixture of conventional centralism and radical reform. It must be said that Thatcherism in practice never fully developed into the market democracy sought by New Right. It is perhaps a fitting epitaph to the Thatcher years to note that the rhetoric soured central–local relations, and that there was only limited policy success over spending, public dissatisfaction over local taxation, and public disinterest over the ideological dispute over municipal provision. The promise of a return to a less conflictual approach was welcome.

The scope of the reforms are the basis of this book. Scotland for once, was catching up with developments in England – where the abolition of the metropolitan counties, VFM auditing, the growth of quangos, and self-governing schools, were all proceeding apace. The result there was described by Butcher *et al.* (1990):

> Once virtually all the major level services in the larger towns and cities were in the hands of the local council. Now these services are distributed between the offices of central government departments or national quasi-government agencies, special purpose authorities, joint boards, and over much of the country two-tiers of elected government. City government has thus become a confusing jumble of overlapping and conflicting jurisdictions of the kind condemned by Goschen a century ago. (1990, p. 21)

Municipal Thatcherism did present a fundamental challenge to the conventional system of local government based on representative democracy and municipal provision; and fully developed, it promised a cheaper, more responsive form of market democracy. Many of the ideas of municipal Thatcherism remained on the Conservative agenda after her loss of power. The *impact*, however, is much less clear, and it is to the evaluation of its development that we now turn.

3 Reforming Local Government Finance

The politics of local spending

Controlling local spending has been a central political objective of British governments since the fiscal crisis of 1976. The election of the first Thatcher administration in 1979 simply served to give added impetus to this concern. Whereas Labour had been almost apologetic to local authorities for requiring expenditure cuts of them, the Conservatives commitment stemmed from ideological belief.

From 1961, all public expenditure – regardless of the source of finance – was planned and controlled within the Public Expenditure Survey, which was originally conceived in a period of low inflation as a means of planning expenditure growth in real terms. The 1976 crisis led to a shift in emphasis from planning to control (Wright, 1980), and cash limits on expenditure totals replaced volume planning whereby automatic compensation for inflation was provided. However, local government finance as a whole was not strictly amenable to cash limits, only those grants provided by central government, as rate-borne expenditure could be used to finance local expenditure above the levels forecast in the Survey. Local government finance was identified as a 'problem' in public expenditure control (Wright, 1977).

Expenditure by local authorities falls into two categories, capital and revenue. Capital expenditure creates an asset bringing long-term benefits to the community, usually in the form of a building (a school, council house or old people's home) but also in terms of infrastructure and plant. As it is financed mainly by borrowing, it has always been accepted by local authorities that central government should have the right to control capital spending levels, for purposes of macro-economic management. For the most part, central government has been able to effect strategic control over capital spending (Midwinter and Monaghan, 1991a).

Revenue expenditure, by contrast, is in respect of day-to-day running costs – staff salaries, heating, and so on – and is financed from user charges, government grants and local taxes. Historically, the right to tax has been regarded as an essential factor in delivering responsive and responsible local government. Arguments for central control over total revenue spending are much less convincing. Indeed, it has only been raised as an issue by central government since 1970. The justification for controls on local taxes is difficult to sustain, as these have no effect on borrowing (Dawson, 1983). The gap between central plans and local budgets has never been great, and in the main has resulted from differing estimates of inflation rather than service spending (Perlman and Lynch, 1979).

Capital expenditure can only be incurred with the consent of the Secretary of State for Scotland. This is effected through the system known as 'Financial Planning'. The Scottish Secretary makes capital allocations to local authorities, based on his assessments of their relative needs, and on their capacity to generate income from council house sales in the case of the housing programme. Within the totals determined, authorities have scope to vire resources between the service programmes.

In terms of the government's concern with spending levels, revenue expenditure has been at the heart of the central–local conflict. Relationships with local government over financial matters are formalised within the working party on local government finance, which is chaired by the Secretary of State for Scotland, but most of the detailed work is delegated to officials in the expenditure committee, the distribution committee and the capital planning committee. The local authority side is led by officials of COSLA, with special advisers from local authorities, mainly from finance, but including some chief executives and planners. The decision-making process culminates in the announcement of capital allocations and the grant levels (known as *aggregate external finance*) for the coming fiscal year.

The smaller Scottish network allows for informality and direct discussions between authorities and the Scottish Office on specific issues. Although local authorities have a common interest in achieving a high level of grant provision, their interests clash over grant distribution, and a number of authorities – for example, Highland, Lothian and Western Isles – have conducted high-profile campaigns over the inadequacy of their needs assessments (known as *grant-aided expenditure assessments*) for grant distribution purposes. Relations between Scotland's local authorities and the Scottish Office have been increasingly tense in the 1980s, exacerbated by growing Labour dominance and Conservative decline in local government. The 1980s witnessed some spectacular conflicts in Edinburgh and Stirling.

Conservative strategy has been to achieve greater economy and efficiency in local government. In terms of economy, they have enhanced the powers inherited from Labour. From 1945 to 1975, political strategy led to higher spending *and* higher grant. Making additional resources available was one way of influencing local authorities to expand provision, for local councillors – contrary to folk wisdom – are generally reluctant to raise local taxes excessively. Labour applied cash limits to the RSG, thereby ensuring that any shortfall would have to be met from local taxes, or spending reduced. In broad terms, Labour's spending targets were met by the local authorities. To assist in this, Labour introduced 'Current Expenditure Guidelines', which gave an indication to each individual authority as to what they ought to spending to be consistent with the government's plans, but acknowledged that: 'the figures are indicative rather than definitive; they are subject to a small margin of error because objective criteria are not available' (Finance Circular No. 75/1976).

The Conservatives sought initially to achieve spending reductions through *grant reductions*. Local authorities made some reductions, but also passed on some of these costs in the form of rates increases. This approach was supplemented by *grant penalties*, whereby authorities which overspent their guidelines lost grant as a result; *rate-capping*, whereby authorities incurring what the government considered to be 'excessive and unreasonable' expenditure had their spending capped; and *financial limits*, which were placed on rate fund contributions to the housing account, and finally eliminated in the reforms of 1988.

By 1986, local spending as a whole had been reduced as a proportion of GDP. Revenue spending had been held broadly stable in volume terms. The degree of overspending had settled at around 3–4 per cent above government plans. The government had argued that the problem had been caused by a minority of left-wing councils, but in fact overspending was more widespread than this (Midwinter *et al.*, 1983). The reality was one of a situation under control, but the political significance of rates – an unpopular tax with the Conservative middle-class – was still a dominant concern. The rating revaluation of 1985 adversely affected some businesses and, more importantly, middle-class home owners in the Conservative heartland (Midwinter *et al.*, 1987). The result was a storm of protest, combining with Mrs Thatcher's hostility to the tax to lead to a commitment to replace rating. An earlier review in 1982 had failed to produce an acceptable alternative, but by 1986 right-wing Thatcherism was more widespread in Conservative circles, and traditional Tory pragmatism and caution was thrown to the wind as a radical reform was proposed.

Until the introduction of the community charge in 1989–90, Conservative strategy had been to transfer the tax burden from central government to local government, thereby enforcing restraint through ratepayer pressures. In the aftermath, the view was that these pressures failed because of inadequacies in the financial system. Local authorities' marginal spending (that is, above needs assessments) was funded by business ratepayers and a minority of citizens, giving incentives to vote for overspending to non-ratepayers. The scope for creative accounting, and the instability of the grant system, further distorted the situation. The solution was to make business rates a national tax, and replace domestic rates with a flat-rate community charge, with rebates for low-income households. This would provide electors with a 'clear incentive to consider the costs and benefits of extra local spending' (DOE, 1991).

The community charge (or poll tax) experiment provides a good example of the dangers of basing public policy on abstract economic arguments. In theory under the community charge system, electors would have to bear directly the cost of voting for 'overspending'; authorities would recognise this and adjust spending downwards. Political analysis of voting behaviour, however, suggests that voters' actions are determined by more complex factors (Miller, 1988). Given the interdependence of central and local government, voters are as likely to attribute blame to the progenitors of the new system as its implementors. For a decade, councils had used 'coping' strategies to contain their spending, in the face of stiff grant penalties. Over the five-year period prior to the poll tax, overspending was between 3 and 4 per cent above government provision. In the first year of the new system, penalties were removed, and spending rose rather than fell – although in part this simply reflected councils restoring budget elements which had been subject to creative accounting. This pattern continued into the second year of the system. No electoral punishment was suffered at the 1990 regional elections by the overspending authorities. Voting patterns continued much as before.

Moreover, the cost to electors rose as the administrative weaknesses of the community charge system became clear. With a dynamic register, an increased volume of taxpayers and a more complex rebate system, the result (as predicted by professionals) was problems of collection, and higher tax bills for payers. Although the government had been forecasting modest levels of taxes, their assumptions were found to be hopelessly inaccurate, and actual bills were around 10 per cent higher (Midwinter and Monaghan, 1991b).

Whatever the theoretical and practical problems of the poll tax, it was the widespread and occasionally violent protest in England that hastened its demise. For Margaret Thatcher, it was to be a flagship of the government, and she steadfastly refused to consider its removal. Michael Heseltine, in challenging her for the Conservative leadership in 1990, made a commitment to review the system, having consistently rejected it as unfair and unworkable. The appointment of John Major as Prime Minister and Heseltine at the Department of the Environment brought the political will to axe a deeply unpopular, financially costly, and short-lived tax system.

The new council tax

The council tax emerged as part of the local government review undertaken by the Department of the Environment and the Scottish and Welsh Offices. Announcing the application of the proposals to Scotland, Scottish Secretary Ian Lang argued that the council tax would be easy to administer, spread the tax burden as widely as possible, and enable councils to remain accountable to their electors (Scottish Office, 1991a). It is the government's view that an appropriate local tax should take account of most adults, be simple and cheap to collect, should demand less from single- person households than larger ones, and should vary within a limited range, according to property values. The consultation paper set out (p. 2) five key principles.

- *Accountability* – Any system should ensure that local people see a link between what they are being asked to pay and what their council is spending.
- *Fairness* – Any tax should be perceived as fair by the public.
- *Ease of collection* – Administrative arrangements for collection and enforcement should be as straightforward as possible.
- *An equitable distribution of the burden* – The principle that most adults should make some contribution has been widely accepted.

- *Restraint* – A system of local taxation should not allow tax bills to become too high either because of unreasonable levels of spending by local authorities or because the system imposes a disproportionately high burden on any any individual or household compared with others.

The key elements of the tax may be summarised briefly:

- households receive a single bill;
- the 'liable person' will usually be the owner or tenant;
- the tax is based on banded capital values;
- the tax assumes a two-adult household;
- there is a separate water charge;
- rebates up to 100 per cent of the tax (excluding the water element) are available to low-income households;
- discounts of 25 per cent accrue to single-person households;
- discounts of 50 per cent apply to dwellings which are not permanent residences – for example, holiday homes;
- discounts of 50 per cent apply where all the adults qualify for a personal discount, as set out in the Act.

The new system eliminates most of the administrative problems which arose from the poll tax. The number of bills is reduced; the problem of councils trying to collect small sums of money from low-income families under the 20 per cent contribution requirement is eliminated; and the requirement to keep track of individuals through a register is removed. Most of the administrative factors which hindered poll tax collection have gone. Collection could have been further eased by restoring the ability of council tenants to pay rent and rates together, but this has not been permitted, presumably because of government beliefs that this obscures accountability.

Although the government refer to the new tax as combining a property element and a personal element, it should be clear that the determining factor is the property element. Properties are allocated to one of eight bands, with the assumption that a two-adult household is the norm. Indeed, 54 per cent of households fall into this category, whereas 33 per cent are single-person and 13 per cent are households with three or more adults. Properties are allocated into one of eight bands and then discounts for single-person households are deducted from the amount due. No account is taken of any adults *above* the two-person norm, but the scale of the discount reflects the banding.

The tax is therefore primarily a property tax, with a discount for single persons. This situation led to the tax being described as 'son of poll tax', or at least its cousin (Local Government Information Unit, 1992), but this is an exaggeration. What the council tax does do is place upper limits for the most valuable houses, and a minimum tax for the least valuable. However, individual households which faced a significant increase in their liability as a result of the transition from community charge to council tax are eligible for transitional relief to dampen the effect until 1995. Enforcement procedures remain broadly the same – reminders, summary warrants, arrestment of earnings and bank accounts, attachment of income support and poindings and warrant sales.

The notion of local accountability depending on the requirement to pay is paid lip service to, in the government's claim that the tax takes account of around 90 per cent of adults – but it would be more accurate to say that it takes account of the 17 per cent of the population living in single-adult households, and for the remainder the liability to pay depends on the property value and household income.

Scottish authorities have had only minor technical teething problems with the council tax. First, this is because the volume of enquiries from taxpayers has fallen dramatically. Secondly, the level of appeals against 'banding' is 50–60 per cent of that pertaining under rates. Thirdly, because local politicians have been more sympathetic to the tax, they have not hesitated to approve the new resources requirement for implementation. Fourthly, payments are being made more timeously than under the community charge, although some public resentment can arise because of the rapidity with which notice of arrears is now triggered. Fifthly, several regions have ended their use of districts as agents, thus permitting the development of a 'one-door' approach compared with the fragmentation of responsibility for registration, billing and collecting under the community charge. Finally, the form of local tax has ceased to be a contentious political issue, with more than half of Scots approving of it (Midwinter, 1993).

The grant and capping system

The changes in tax system required only minor modifications to the grant system. The practice of distributing grant to support standard spending for a standard level of tax continues, compensating for variations in needs and taxable capacity. *Grant Aided Expenditure* (GAE), the Scottish equivalent of Standard Spending Assessments, continues to be based on a client group approach. Expenditure needs for services and components of service are determined mainly by a primary indicator, usually in the form of a population-based client group, with adjustments for secondary indicators which are weighted through regression analysis with past spending. Any marginal spending above the standard GAE falls wholly on local taxpayers. This approach was recently described as one of the most sophisticated fiscal equalisation systems in Europe (CSL, 1993), but it retains the same weaknesses as it did under the community charge (Keating and Midwinter, 1993). That is, a proper attempt to cost a standard level of service would begin by defining the standard, and then calculate the cost of achieving it. Under GAE, the approach is to determine a level of expenditure, allocate it on the basis of incidence of social indicators, and *assume* that this equates to the cost of a standard service. As under poll tax, therefore, a council spending at GAE would not necessarily provide a standard service, nor, because of the availability of balances or other financial assumptions made, would it necessarily levy a standard tax.

This brings us neatly to the new capping system, which has been brought into line with the English and Welsh system. The consultation paper argued that:

> capping will be important during the transition to the new system, when local accountability will inevitably be clouded by the changes in the local government finance system and by the phasing in of new bills. It will avoid the risk of a repeat of the substantial increase in spending which accompanied the transition to the community charge. (DoE, 1991, p. 25)

Under rates and the community charge, the capping powers applied to councils which, in the Secretary of State's judgement, were proposing 'excessive and unreasonable' expenditure, and which had their rates capped as a result. Under the council tax, capping applies to budget increases as well as excessive spending compared with GAE. The result is in effect a system of 'universal capping', whereby spending increases are limited for all authorities, depending on their existing budget and its relationship to its GAE. The alleged practice of using Scotland as a 'guinea-pig' for subsequent English legislation has been clearly reversed in this case.

Table 3.1 *Comparison of local budgets and government assessments in Scotland*

Year	Excess %	Number of authorities in excess
1988–89	3.8	33
1989–90	7.4	28
1990–91	5.4	25
1991–92	2.5	29
1992–93	1.2	39
1993–94	2.2	30

Source: Rating Review.

Table 3.1 records the gap between authorities' budgets and GAE provision, showing the government's success in restraining expenditure since 1989–90, although several authorities had to resort to creative accounting to achieve acceptable budgets, and stress is beginning to show with the increased excess in 1993–94.

But what of accountability? The Scottish Secretary made it plain to the local authorities that they would now be accountable to him, and that he would be more rigorous than local electors. Concern for accountability has been a recurring theme in local government finance since Layfield. That report argued that there was a need for financial arrangements to reflect the desired pattern of relations, with the guiding principle being that whichever party determined expenditure should have responsibility for raising the necessary taxation.

The government's preferred solutions have to some extent followed Layfield's arguments. Reducing grant was seen as a way of delivering local accountability and lower spending. Then it was a public choice approach though the poll tax (Bailey, 1990; Barnett and Knox, 1992), although this reform *increased* the degree of central control through in effect transforming non-domestic rates into a national tax. Now, it has gone further, with high levels of central taxation and expenditure limits – a centralist solution. This makes the reference to 'local accountability' in the consultation paper difficult to comprehend. This appears to mean the need to levy a local tax and little more. Given the continuing complications of the grant system and the broad-based nature of client group assessments, the public will no more be able to make the link between spending and local taxation than before, given the emphasis on spending increases rather than taxation as the determinant of capping. For example, in 1991–92, Stirling was the only council in Scotland not to increase its poll tax, yet it increased its spending by 7 per cent.

The new arrangements are a new centralism, consistent with the government's fiscal strategy and obsession with local government finance. It is no longer consistent with the public choice analysis which underpinned the poll tax. The reality is that since the introduction of capping in the early 1980s, Conservative strategy has been about the achievement of control, and even the poll tax aberration was with the specific objective of delivering spending reductions. The result is a reduced choice for citizens, as local authorities' scope for action is limited by central government. Local government now has reduced responsibility and discretion (Jones, 1977). Traditionally, that discretion has been achieved through statutes which provide for it, and through local taxation which gave a degree of autonomy beyond central government spending plans. Local government no longer has fiscal accountability to its electors, yet consistently, those electors regard the case for fiscal controls as weak (Midwinter and Monaghan, 1993).

As a system of taxation, the council tax does have the requirements of a local tax. It has a stable yield, it is visible, and cheap to collect. The new centralism results *not* from fiscal reform, but from the extension of capping. Arguments for a higher level of locally-based finance continue to be made (Audit Commission, 1991) but of itself that matters less than the capping controls. The traditional fiscal autonomy of local government has been eroded, the reforms are centralising, and no convincing economic or political case for such change has been made.

The new financial orthodoxy

The government has also focused its attention on budgetary practice within local government. The Scottish Accounts Commission acquired value-for-money (VFM) powers in 1988. This also provided the Accounts Commission with a 'requirement' to ensure that local authorities make proper arrangements for ensuring economy, efficiency and effectiveness. The traditional role of the local authority auditor has been to examine the legality and regularity of expenditure. The VFM role breaks new ground, and in a field in which expertise is not particularly well developed.

VFM became the new financial orthodoxy of the 1980s (Holtham and Stewart, 1981). The development of performance indicators (PIs) in particular appeared to offer the sharp edge equivalent to markets in the private sector. In practice, this reflects the relative ease of setting and monitoring PIs, however ill-defined, inappropriate or inadequate. Attention has been focused by practitioners on PIs, as the most tangible aspect of VFM analysis. The Accounts Commission itself gave a high profile to the derivation of performance indicators. In the changed political context of Thatcherism, the political clout required to ensure development took place was seen to be on hand. Management consultants hyped the potential for performance measurement by issuing their own 'hands-on' guides (Butt and Palmer, 1985). As Carter (1991) observed, the government was breathing new life into old ideas, with unprecedented enthusiasm.

In Scotland, the Accounts Commission provided guidance as to what it considered proper arrangements for achievement of economy, efficiency and effectiveness. These were:

- existence of commitment and corporate approach to VFM within an authority, for example, steering group or performance review mechanism;
- definition and quantification of attainable objectives;
- derivation of performance indicators and subsequent monitoring of actual performance;
- incidence of reviews of particular service and activity levels and related costs and outputs;
- evidence of periodic external comparison with the costs and performance applying in the private sector for all appropriate services and activities;
- maintenance of adequate procedures to ensure optimum utilisation of scarce resources;
- existence of adequate management information, that is, accurate, timeous and made available in appropriate detail to levels of accountable management.   (Accounts Commission, 1988)

This model indeed bears the hallmarks of past reforms, although it lacks the emphasis on strategic/corporate goals characteristic of Planning Programming Budgetary Systems or corporate planning models (Dearlove, 1979). The resemblance is strong enough to raise doubts about its practicability. Previous attempts at performance measurement were not particularly successful (Greenwood and

Stewart, 1974; Skelcher, 1980). The first survey of Scottish practice revealed that little progress had been made in the first four years: a majority of authorities had no staff specifically dealing with VFM matters (68 per cent); had no written statement of objectives; and did not make use of performance indicators in budget allocation and control (84 per cent) (Midwinter and Monaghan, 1993). Does this reflect a gap between theory and practice?

The notion that there is a better, more rational way of allocating resources in government is a seductive concept. In the 1980s, more so than the 1970s, there was a political concern to improve efficiency. The *Financial Management Initiative* (FMI), launched in 1982, introduced these ideas into central departments. FMI was the intended mechanism whereby each department had an organisation and a system in which managers at all levels have:

- a clear view of these objectives, and means to assess and wherever possible, measure outputs or performance in relating to those objectives;
- well-defined responsibility for making the best use of their resources, including a critical scrutiny of output and value-or-money; and
- the information (particularly about costs) the training and the access to expert advice that they need to exercise their responsibilities effectively. (HM Treasury, 1982)

At the centre of this philosophy lies the accounting concept of value-for-money in financial management. The accountancy field sees the issue very much as a narrow, organisational one rather than an element of budgetary politics.

The impression is given of a simple and direct link between objective-setting and performance, in a world characterised by a lack of complexity. It is a normative model:

To obtain decision-making of the *highest quality* [my emphasis] it is necessary to provide appropriate information and finance has spurned a wide variety of information sources that can help. These include annual financial statements, audit reports, periodic budget statements and *ad hoc* performance reports, all incorporating an appropriate package of financial performance indicators. (Tonge, 1992, p. 81)

It is financial information as a representation of organisational behaviour, activity and decision-making which provides a common thread acting as a link between the various elements. To that end, financial management is the process and techniques which link delegated financial responsibility to financial accountability.   (ibid., p. 80).

The VFM approach utilises three central concepts:

- *economy* – which refers to limitations of inputs;
- *efficiency* – which maps the ratio of inputs to outputs; and
- *effectiveness* – the meeting of objectives.

This approach requires the development of performance indicators for evaluative purposes, and to allow the decentralisation of resource management to managers within a framework of 'hands off' control (Carter, 1991, p. 87). This approach would also permit a systematic approach to problem solving through a clear emphasis on outputs and objectives (Jackson, 1988).

Performance assessment is not, however, unproblematic, and difficulties abound in actually defining performance and measuring outputs. Official accounts of the need and scope for performance measurement usually record such problems, but do not regard them as insurmountable. A member of the Audit Commission staff gives the flavour of this view in a recent publication. Henderson-Stewart (1988) argues that effective performance review has 'always' been critical to the management of a local authority, but councils must now 'shift' their emphasis to monitoring and reviewing outputs. Though there are 'genuine difficulties in defining and measuring outputs', this is no reason to avoid 'explicit review'. Thus:

> The Commission therefore believes it is a disservice to local govern-
> ment to dwell too much on the theoretical difficulties of measuring
> performance. What is more useful is to propose practical ways in
> which local authorities actually can measure their performance.
> (p. 109)

Henderson-Stewart goes on to argue against 'an exclusive emphasis on financial measures', but for the need to give a 'prominent place to costs'. Costs and levels of service provision *are by themselves inadequate*, and the most critical indicator is the 'value or benefit' to the user. He does not, however, go on to tackle the issue of value measurement, merely to note that past failure to tackle 'effectiveness' is not a reason to 'abandon performance measurement', but to ensure that 'quality and effectiveness' are tackled. Tell us how ! The VFM approach is justified on the basis of 'management theory', which is presumed to state 'that every activity should have explicit targets for it'. Now such a view may be central to the scientific management approach, but management theory in general is far less omnipotent. In short, all the conceptual and measurement problems are acknowledged, but skipped over as if good intentions are enough.

Advocates of PIs play down the problems on the grounds that something is better than nothing. History does not support that view. Reform in the USA in the 1970s showed that there were real problems of analysis in the use of PIs. These were:

- differing objectives mean that organisations have differing performance indicators;
- the degree to which inputs can be directly related to output varies from organisation to organisation;
- the number of objectives pursued by each organisation varies greatly; making the allocations of resources to each problematic;
- the pay-back time for different policies varies greatly. (*Source*: 1970 Report to President and Congress of the Joint Financial Management Improvement Programme [Washington DC: office of Management and Budget, General Accounting Office and Civil Service Commission])

Designing a workable system of PIs is a difficult task. The US experience is not promising, where evaluation in practice was limited to the simplest. Research into practice in central government corroborates this view. There are difficulties in developing effectiveness indicators in particular (Pollitt, 1985); in relating these to resource allocation; and in convincing practitioners of their value (Pollitt, 1985; HM Treasury, 1986). The growth of PIs in the public domain should not be taken as evidence of organisational impact, which is what counts (Carter, 1988). There is considerable dependence on 'availability', and many are either manpower, financial or cardboard statistics. In a quite devastating critique, Harrison (1989) challenges the whole basis of the approach:

what is not clear . . . is just how such information in practice is assisting public sector managers to find better ways of providing services. Across such a broad spectrum of organisations as the public sector presents, generalisations are hazardous, but despite the efforts that have been made, the answer so far must be – *not much* [my emphasis].

Developing VFM in Scotland

The issue of VFM studies was first raised in the Working Party on Local government Finance (the Scottish equivalent of CCLGF) in late 1986, when it was proposed by the Scottish Office that the Accounts Commission should have a major role in its development, drawing on the work of the Audit Commission. The subsequent legislation gave the Accounts Commission the statutory duty to undertake or promote comparative and other studies designed to enable it to make recommendations for improving economy, efficiency and effectiveness in the provision of local services.

In subsequent discussions of the working party, the government challenged the traditional incremental budgetary approach, advocating systematic VFM reviews. These would not be concerned solely with savings, but would also be a way of maintaining service levels at lower cost. There was a recognition that the actual savings being delivered on the ground were much lower than the Audit Commission's projections in England, but a target of at least £10 million per annum for Scotland was suggested, and subsequently this assumption has been built into grant settlements. Studies of scope for savings in refuse collection, janitorial and cleaning provision in schools, and energy management followed.

In 1991, attention focused more strongly on the development of performance indicators through a joint COSLA/Accounts Commission VFM Liaison Group which sought to: 'consider and promote the concept of performance measurement and the application of performance indicators' (Accounts Commission, 1991a, p. 8). This group sought to discover the extent to which VFM type initiatives were underway. This research showed that the majority of authorities had not developed performance indicators, and only half had accepted the 'concept', and concluded that authorities' priorities for developing VFM were:

- the establishment and development of performance standards/ targets and review process;
- the establishment of clear and quantified policy objectives;
- the securing of member/chief officer/staff commitment. (Accounts Commission, 1991b, p. 11)

Political commitment to the Citizen's Charter enhanced the role of the Accounts Commission in these matters. The Local Government Act 1992 required the Commission:

- to give such directions as it thinks fit to each local authority to publish, annually, information as to its standards of performance; and
- to provide the indicators to measure the performance of local authority services – indicators that will (in its opinion) facilitate comparisons of cost, economy, efficiency and effectiveness – from one authority to another and over time.

The Commission has recorded the development of PIs in a series of 'Focus on VFM' papers. In these, they make a number of caveats. First, there is a degree of selectivity. Some service areas have been excluded, and the proposed indicators were not intended to provide comprehensive coverage of all service activities. However, the Commission took the view that these indicators did to some extent measure the '3 Es', although the measurement of effectiveness was less well addressed. Secondly, the Commission recognised problems of comparability, in terms of data consistency, and saw the need to produce *general and service specific context statements* which will assist interpretation of indicators.

The Commission published its Audit Guide for Financial Year 1993–94, which continued to recognise the limitations of the art and identified the need for refinement of indicators. It particularly stressed that citizen evaluation of authorities' performance is unscientific and imprecise, and cannot be reduced to a series of indicators.

Problems of methodology

Although less ambitious than some of its managerialist predecessors, the model is clearly a descendant of systems such as Management by

Objectives (MBO), and Planning Programming Budgetary Systems (PPBS), systems imbued with the ideas of rational choice. It is seldom acknowledged by the advocates of such systems that their central concepts were derived from what is essentially an idealised model of decision-making, whereas real world decision-making is characterised by 'bounded rationality' (Simon, 1958) or even 'muddling through' (Lindblom, 1959). Problems of setting objectives and measuring outputs are well recorded. Indeed, the rational model is so technically complex and information hungry as to be totally impractical as a basis for public policy- making (Leach, 1982). Although the performance review model admits to lacking comprehensiveness, it still operates on the assumption that ends and means are distinct. The lessons of experience are all ignored (Wildavsky, 1979). The Accounts Commission model sets out links between:

Objectives

↓

Policies

↓

Performance Indicators

↓

Targets

Compared with the definition of PPBS given below, the intellectual inheritance is clear enough. PPBS was seen to be:

> A management system for an organisation as a whole, providing regular procedures for reviewing goals and objectives, for selecting and planning programmes over a period of years in terms of output related both to the objective and to resources necessary to achieve them, for allocating resources between programmes and controlling their implementation.   (Jones and Pendlebury, 1984, p. 75)

Performance review is seen as a central concept in the corporate framework of local authority management. Unfortunately, few authorities actually operate such a framework!

The performance assessment model is replete with problems of conceptualisation and comparability. The first of these relates to the *concept* of a PI itself. Put simply, the model lacks a set of tests that need to be met for acceptance as a PI. There is reference to the criteria of cost, economy, efficiency and effectiveness, but even these concepts are not rigorously applied. The Commission's definition of these concepts is set out in Figure 3.1, but in contrast with the definitional criteria used for selecting need indicators for grant distribution, the framework is unsystematic. In the RSG, indicators are only acceptable as measures of expenditure need when they are:

- plausible;
- outside the control of the local authority; and
- related to past expenditure patterns.

Such indicators are deemed to be reflective of the authorities' need to spend on specific services. It is assumed that the past expenditure patterns between authorities differ for reasons of need; cost; policy choice; and efficiency. Efficiency is assumed to be a residual element, not related systematically to past spending. In the case of performance assessment, we are seeking to explain variations in efficiency. It is therefore crucial that the indicators used do reflect the performance of the organisation, and that these cannot be influenced by environmental factors in the same way that local authority policy choice can influence spending variations. Such factors should be systematically excluded, but in the present model, are simply to be set out as context descriptors: 'features of the external environment in which the organisation operates, or inherent characteristics of tenants, applicants, clients, claimants, etc. which the organisation could not be expected to control'. By contrast, a PI is regarded as a 'measure or commentary on *how successful the management and operational service delivery of the organisation is,* and for which it can be legitimately held accountable'. (Accounts Commission, 1992) How well do the measures used meet this definition? The answer is, not very well at all. The indicators can be grouped in five categories as shown in Figure 3.2 and Table 3.2.

Despite the acknowledged inadequacy of 'cost' measures, nearly half of the statistics are simply financial statistics. They do not even measure 'economy' in terms of the definition used in Figure 3.3. Spending by client group in social work, per pupil in education, or on types of road maintenance, tells us nothing *per se* about value-for-money. The measures of success, such as crime clear-up rates, repairs meeting standards, or the percentage of the population served by public sewers, do not of *themselves* indicate organisational efficiency.

Figure 3.1   *Performance review in context*

Where are we going?	*Aims and Strategy* *Statement* Mission and values	
		Policy Review Performance Reviews
What do we need?	*Service Plans* Needs Resources	
How do we expect to get there?	*Budgets and Targets* Action Plans Performance Outcomes	
Making it happen	*Monitoring* Standards of performance Targets Performance appraisal Performance measures	
Have we got there?	*Annual Results* Service targets Strategic targets Resource targets Assessment	
Getting better	*Replan*	

Table 3.2 *Type of performance indicator (PI)*

Type	Number
Financial statistics	45
Success rate statistics	9
Service statistics	14
User statistics	10
Response time statistics	16
Total	94

Figure 3.2 *Selected performance indicators (PIs)*

Financial statistics

- Spending per pupil (education)
- spending per client (social work)
- spending on maintenance (roads)
- water supply charges
- sewerage charges
- tenant arrears

Service statistics

- percentage of qualified staff in residence homes.
- number of inspections per annum
- number of libraries/opening hours.

Success rate statistics

- percentage waste recycled
- percentage crimes cleared up
- percentage repairs completed to standard

Response time statistics

- processing claims
- processing council house sales
- processing planning applications.

User statistics

- client numbers
- percentage population served by public services
- average attendance per opening hours.

Figure 3.3   *Measures of performance*

Measures

Costs	*Resources*	*Outputs*	*Outcome*
resource costs	staff	services	impact of
service costs	buildings	delivered	Outputs
	equipment, etc.	products	value user benefits

Indicators

Economy	*Efficiency*	*Effectiveness*
Costs related to:	Outputs related to:	Outcomes related to:
Resources	*Inputs*	*Objectives*
the purchase or provision of services at the lowest possible cost consistent with a specified quality and quantity of service.	the provision of a specified volume and quality of service with the lowest level of resources capable of meeting that specification.	providing the services which allow the organisation to implement polices and achieve its objectives.

Variations could reflect geographic/environmental factors, which, though set out as context descriptors, are not related to the indicators in any systematic way. Similar points could be made about measures of user patterns, or response/processing times.

This makes it very difficult in most instances to draw any causal connection between organisational efficiency and the indicators used. The incidence of intervening variables makes proper comparison between authorities problematic. Nevertheless, there is a bigger problem which is not recognised in official circles. It is that these indicators are supposed to be indicative of the success of the local authorities in meeting their policy objectives. In practice, this is not considered at all. Rather, a simple set of measures is assumed to provide the basis of comparison between authorities *irrespective* of their policy objectives. For example, variations in income generation, house reletting times, assessment times or class size, could *all* reflect differences of policy rather than efficiency. Such measures could not possibly provide the basis of valid inter-authority comparisons unless authorities had the same policies. The statistics in the main do not measure performance against policy objectives.

The implications for practice

The conventional wisdom is to recognise some of these data limitations and methodological problems, and argue for refinement. Yet the problems referred to are not new: they reflect the same analytical and conceptual constraints faced by the intellectual predecessors of the VFM approach. The advocates of PPBS in the USA regularly exhorted the service departments to 'clarify goals, define objectives and relate these to quantitative indicators', but could never actually demonstrate how it should be done' (Wildavsky, 1979, p. 194). It is not being unkind to point out the lack of progress with 'refinement' in Britain. This does not reflect failure of the 'practitioners'. *The problem is with the model, and its imposition on the bureaucracy by the political process.* The 'indicators' are not indicators at all, but the best that can be produced in the complex world of public service provision, where qualitative judgements over individual and community needs continuously require to be made. The notion that authorities' performance can be reduced to a few simple, quantifiable indicators which form the basis for comparison of organisational efficiency is fallacious. It is clear that quality and effectiveness assessment through indicators is no closer to attainment than it was in the 1960s. It is also clear that the indicators of economy and efficiency are also inadequate for the purposes intended. The basis for sensible and equitable comparison between authorities does not yet exist, and therefore the statutory requirement to undertake comparison on the basis of limited information ought to be withdrawn.

Secondly, the data generated in the public domain should be reclassified as simply *local government statistics*. The application of the term 'performance indicator' is not justifiable in the current state of the art. However, the statistics would be of use for internal policy analysis in assisting councils to reach decision on budgetary priorities or service development. But that requires the statistics to be placed in an interpretative context which also consider social needs. Under the VFM legislation, the Accounts Commission cannot question policy, yet it is precisely as sources of data for policy analysis that such statistics could serve a useful purpose, for 'analysis evaluates and sifts alternative means and ends in the elusive pursuit of policy recommendations' (Wildavsky, 1964, p. 190).

VFM analysis, by deliberately excluding questions of policy, is destined to be of limited value to local government. Regrettably, the Accounts Commission remit leaves it concerned with evaluating the 'policy arrangements' against the standards of the wholly unrealistic criteria of the rational model.

> It is *not* the auditor's function to question policy. It is, however, a valid exercise of his role both to consider the effects of policy and to examine the arrangements by which policy decisions are reached, implemented and reviewed. This will entail for example, his consideration of –
>
> - whether policy objectives have been determined, and policy decisions taken with appropriate authority;
> - whether established policy aims and objectives have been clearly set out;
> - the extent to which policy objectives are set, and decisions based, on sufficient, relevant and reliable financial and other data, and with the critical underlying assumptions made explicit; and
> - whether there are satisfactory arrangements for considering alternative options, including the identification, selection and evaluation of such options.   (Accounts Commission, 1991a, p. 12)

Comparing local authority decision-making in practice against the standards of an ideal-type model will fail to provide potential for progress. The dislike of incrementalism, with its focus on marginal change, is central to the advocacy of the rational approach. The evidence of empirical research is that rationality is at best a superficial model, which bears no relationship to how decisions are or could be taken in local government (Elcock *et al.*, 1989). Progress will only be made with recognition of the major conceptual and political constraints on rationality which make it an inappropriate prescriptive model. Bureaucratic models of this type have unsuccessful pedigrees.

It would be better to recognise this now before disillusionment and defeatism become widespread, and allow auditors to concentrate on tasks for which they are competent, and have the technology – the traditional audit role – rather than undertaking the flawed calculus of value-for-money. At the moment, practice reflects a superficial concern with the terminology of VFM, at the expense of critical and rigorous appraisal, in pursuit of limited political objectives. There is, a case, however, for authorities utilising PIs within an internal approach to budgetary review, but this can be carried out in recognition of the limitations of the art and the need for qualitative judgment. Performance indicators are only tools for use in such budgetary review, not determinants of decisions. They may lead to no more than asking 'why' such differences occur and finding acceptable explanations for the authority. In context, they can assist decision-making. Page (1989) has argued that they are misleading and unhelpful tools of political analysis between institutions. This will not prevent them being used in political debate when they support an ideological position. In practice, however, their scope for application is more limited, their relevance varies with services and types of indicator, and their purpose should be to *assist* decision-making, not determine it.

Conclusion

The government's reforms have secured stability and control in local government finance. Local authorities now raise only a small proportion of their income from local taxation. Their budgets are set in a tight framework of fiscal control which severely limits local autonomy. Government strategy still places emphasis on efficiency savings, but these are not being delivered in the true sense of the word. Local authorities are still engaging in creative accountancy and budget trimming rather than efficiency savings. The VFM framework has had only a limited impact. The technology for sensible comparison of performance remains crude, and fraught with conceptual problems.

The new framework does meet the government's *control* objectives, if not its efficiency ones. The tight framework, however, will put the onus on government in the changeover to the new system – to deliver a grant settlement which controls costs without damaging services in the transition. That juggling act remains a delicate balance.

4 Privatising Municipal Provision

Public choice analysis

We noted earlier the growing importance of public choice theory in Conservative political philosophy. Although derived from economics, in its application of economic concepts to the analysis of democracy and bureaucracy, it is the support it provided to the Conservative case for political reform of local government that renders its understanding important.

The approach is the development of a positive model of politics through deductive reasoning, based on the assumption that economic rationality is sufficiently pervasive in political behaviour to allow economic predictions – usually about local spending growth – to be made. Maximising behaviour by bureaucrats and politicians is seen to result in the oversupply of public goods . Part of the problem is the structure of the political market place. On the supply side, rational bureaucrats seek to maximise budgets, and are assisted in this through the budgeting structure, whereby a professional department is 'supervised' by an executive committee – what Niskanen (1971) calls a 'passive sponsor' – wholly dependent on the information provided by the professional manager as the basis of budgetary choice. Because of the absence of a direct link between paying and consuming, electors consistently vote for higher levels of spending and services than they would do if they had to pay for this consumption as customers.

The realism of these assumptions has been subject to considerable criticism. Politicians pursue political values and policies, bureaucrats are not all budget maximisers (Dunleavy, 1979; Kogan 1973), and the logic of the argument that rational behaviour leads to oversupply ignores the competing force of services where benefits are broadly spread rather than concentrated on particular interest groups. The result is more likely to be mis-supply (Goodin, 1982).

Normative public choice (Gibson, 1987), however, develops a series of policy instruments for tackling these perceived weaknesses, including privatisation, competition, consumer choice through vouchers, and direct charging for services (Niskanen, 1971). The limitations of deductive reasoning as a basis for public policy have been recognised by Jackson (1989), who argued that the complexity of real-life policymaking required more than policies based upon simple axioms and maxims. For the political New Right, however, such assumptions are taken as givens. Public choice theorists 'have shown' that people behave in politics as they do in economics (Pirie, 1988). Applying public choice theory, they proceed to advocate competitive tendering as an alternative to direct municipal provision:

> We need members and officials who are not wedded to the power base of a large department; who do not believe that success is measured by the number of staff they employ and the amount of money they spend; who are not prisoners of any pressure group; who are not overinfluenced by the unions or other producer groups. (Ridley, 1988, p. 29)

Market efficiency in the absence of full privatisation, should be enhanced by surrogate forms, to provide for some equivalent to the control they see exercised by the public over the private sector. Such blind faith ignores the reality of monopolistic provision and the absence of private competition in many markets (Galbraith, 1973), and moreover simply asserts there will be beneficial impact of such policy changes. Pirie (1992) notes the links between privatisation, internal markets, and the Citizen's Charter:

> The common thread linking the three policies is Public Choice Theory. They arise from a desire to make society interactive and spontaneous instead of command driven, but the methods they choose are specifically limited to an analysis of society which applies the methods of economics to social affairs. Public Choice Theory uses the premise that politicians, civil servants, interest groups and ordinary electors behave as if they were economic participants, each trying to maximize their advantage, and acting continually to serve their objectives . . .

> The policies which are formulated in the light of Public Choice Theory are more complex and more sophisticated than their rivals precisely because they take account of interest groups and attempt to circumvent the opposition which might be generated by them in the normal course of events. (Pirie, 1992, pp. 14 and 15).

The end result is assumed to be greater citizen choice – although no empirical examination of the actual impact of such policies is offered. Markets, competition choice and accountability are self-evidently related for the New Right. Thatcherite politicians certainly utilise public choice analysis (Ridley, 1973; Lawson, 1981) in defining 'oversupply' as a problem of tax financed public provision. Its application to local government led Nicholas Ridley to advocate an 'enabling role' for local authorities.

Central to his thesis is again the uncritical assumption of the benefits of competition as a spur to efficiency and value-for-money, based on the experience of a handful of radical right-wing English authorities – which Ridley clearly regarded as heroic:

> At the other end of the spectrum there are Conservative authorities which have taken up the challenge of accountability and competition. They have scrutinized every service and introduced competition. They have disposed of unproductive assets to those who can use them better. They have sought out ways to encourage the private sector and to stimulate the local economy. They have kept closely in touch with the needs and wishes of local people, they have improved services and reduced rate burdens.   (Ridley, 1988, p. 3)

VFM studies and contracting out have shown the scope for savings in local government which exists, and thus to the need for a fundamental shift in the role of local government, away from universal provider, towards 'a key role in ensuring that there is adequate provision to meet needs' (p. 17), and that competitive tendering will 'guarantee the customer value-for-money (p. 21), in a system in which local authorities 'organise, secure and monitor the provision of services, without necessarily providing them themselves' (p. 22).

Ridley's approach is based on certain fundamental political beliefs. These are:

- the greater efficiency of the private sector over the public sector;
- that competition of itself brings benefits;
- the need to challenge the monopoly power of public bureaucracies and public sector trades unions;
- the primacy of individuals as consumers rather than citizens;
- that democracy itself is a constraint on achieving greater efficiency.

Given the prominence paid to local government in traditional Conservatism this appears surprising at first. But it should be remembered that local discretion was seen as a counterbalance to an expanding welfare state centralism, whereas now it is seen as a hindrance to welfare state decline. The New Right are not simply seeking to make local service provision more efficient, they are seeking to redefine democracy, and central to this is an implicit belief that municipal provision is not in the interests of the individual. Thus: 'Central government's preferred policy is to reduce local political power and increase the power of the individual citizen as (non-political) consumer of local services operating within a private market or pseudo-market framework' (Bailey, 1992, p. 7).

We chose the term 'privatisation' as an umbrella term for the policy. Although it has several elements (Pirie, 1985), in the local government sense it refers to a range of policy instruments designed to stimulate market mechanisms in local services. We do not know of any experiment of full-scale privatisation, whereby local government withdraws from service provision and leaves it to the private sector and individual consumers. Indeed, given the statutory context of local government, such an option is difficult to foresee in practice. It is also the case that the privatisation strategy is part of a broader fiscal strategy to reduce public spending (Stoker, 1988). It is also arguable that the limited impact of more conventional fiscal controls in itself stimulated the development of privatising municipal provision.

User charges is one way of reforming what economists call the 'demand-side'. As part of the critique of the inherent defects of municipal provision is that it consists of bureaucratic resource allocation rather than consumer choice, an important element of the political strategy has been to increase that degree of choice. Greater choice in education, housing and community care is prominent. Le Grand describes this as a quasi-market approach:

All these developments thus involve the introduction of quasi-markets into the welfare state. They are 'markets' because they replace monolithic state providers with competitive independent ones. They are 'quasi' because they differ from conventional markets in a number of key ways. The differences are on both the supply and the demand sides. On the supply side, as with conventional markets, there is competition between productive enterprises or service suppliers . . . On the demand side, consumer purchasing power is not expressed in money terms. (Le Grand, 1990, p. 5)

In the remainder of this chapter, we examine the development of quasi-markets in local government, concentrating on empirical analysis of their scope and impact rather than the philosophical issues they raise. Do they in fact improve efficiency, choice, and control as their advocates maintain?

Extending competition

Direct provision of a service by a local authority has been the normal mode of service delivery in local government. This arose not for any ideological reason, but in the absence of private provision of a range of services. Private provision of services, however, is not new and has always played a minor role in local government, particularly in construction work, and can be termed 'contracting out':

> The term 'contracting out' describes the situation where one orga-nisation contracts with another for the provision of a particular form of procurement in the sense that contractors may be considered 'suppliers', but in common usage it has come to refer more specifi-cally to the purchase of an end product which would otherwise be provided 'in-house' by the purchaser himself. (Ascher, 1987, p. 7)

Ascher lists costs, expertise, overhead reductions, convenience and flexibility as reasons why private companies contract out. In the public sector, it is quite common for the purchase of goods – but the new emphasis is on contracting services. Politically, it has been pushed by New Right politicians in the interests of efficiency, believing that competition and private provision of themselves will achieve that.

Ascher traces the origins of compulsory competitive tendering (CCT) to the 1978 'winter of discontent' and the strike by refuse disposal workers. Actions by individual councils, however, were usually a response to problems of industrial relations as much as ideology. Stimulus to change came from the publications of the Adam Smith Institute, and the activities of Michael Forsyth – later to be a government minister – as propagandist and lobbyist. Adopting a public choice critique, Forsyth described public bureaucracies as 'self interested' and uneconomic because the combination of a protected monopoly position with a claim on tax revenues removes all incentive for efficiency of operation and quality of service. (Forsyth, 1980). Democratic control was inadequate, market accountability clearly preferable. When Wandsworth leader Christopher Chope – another fervent privateer – was elected with Forsyth to the House of Commons in 1983, the advocacy of CCT attained a much higher profile (Ascher, 1987).

Scotland was less fertile ground for such ideas, in part due to its stronger 'public sector ethos' (Kerley and Wynn, 1990). Both temperamentally and ideologically, Scottish councils had little liking for the New Right agenda, often seeing it as an alien culture being imposed on more pragmatic Scots. Labour councillors in particular had a commitment to oppose CCT to protect local authority jobs. The logic of CCT required a major cultural shift for authorities from 'employers' and 'guardians of service' to 'clients' dealing with 'contractors'. The very concepts themselves smack of superficiality, given the existence of direct labour organisations or direct service organisations within the local authorities. Philosophically, it is the reduction of resource allocation to issues of simple market efficiency which sits uneasily with the Scottish collective psyche. 'The legislation requires that most of the non-commercial public policy objectives which local authorities have hitherto sought to achieve in the mechanisms through which they actually deliver their services are marginalised . . . (Kerley and Wynn, 1990, p. 7).

Most councillors come into local government concerned with such public policy issues (for example, employing people with disabilities; equality for women;) as well as service delivery. To reduce their role to merely awarding contracts to the cheapest tender was bound to lead to organisational conflict. In contrast with southern England, voluntary contracting out was little pursued in Scotland, although tendering had been used for

primarily the peripheral and low-volume specialist and support services . . . Despite increasing Ministerial support for such a form of service delivery in the Scottish public sector, it took the compulsion of legislation before it was introduced in Scotland, and then in an inevitably different spirit. Instead of dealing with willing clients for their cleansing or catering services, private contractors were faced with public bodies which, in general, resented their approaches and did what they could within the law to see that they were unsuccessful in tendering. (Kerley and Wynn, 1990, p. 8)

Policy developments north and south of the border have proceeded apace. The first legislation was in the 1980 Local Government Planning and Land Act, which introduced competition for housing repairs, highway maintenance and sewerage agency work. Some larger authorities had direct labour organisations (DLOs) to carry out such work. In terms of organisation theory, this can bring advantages of scale, where the volume of work is significant enough to merit full-time staff. But this was also an area where considerable private sector expertise existed and, in the economic slump of the early 1980s, was eager to contract for such work, possibly at competitive prices. The Act required a DLO to earn a 5 per cent rate of return on its capital employed, and to put a proportion of its work out to tender, a proportion which increased over time. The result was a reduction in DLO staffing levels and income of around 20 per cent by 1985 (Stoker, 1988, p. 219).

In February 1985, the government produced a consultation paper – *Competition in the Provision of Local Authority Services*, which proposed compulsory competitive tendering for a list of defined activities, and to end local authority contract compliance policies – an arrangement whereby an authority would pursue social and economic objectives with companies as a condition of being awarded council contracts. The defined activities were:

- refuse collection;
- cleaning of buildings;
- street and other cleansing;
- schools and welfare catering;
- other catering;
- ground maintenance;
- vehicle repair maintenance.

The Act also placed accounting requirements on direct service organisation (DSOs).

- A separate trading account must be set up for each activity and each financial year.
- Financial objectives set by the Secretary of State must be met.
- The objectives would be a required return on capital or on turnover whichever was judged to be more appropriate.
- An annual report for each activity for each financial year must be sent to the authority's auditor and to the Secretary of State.

- The auditor will give the Secretary of State a written opinion on whether the financial objectives have been met.
- Authorities must supply interested parties with the financial provisions of the bids submitted by the DLO and those contractors invited to bid. (Scottish Local Government Information Unit [SLGIU], 1988).

These services are all in areas of manual work. The extension to public cleansing services was not surprising, given past problems of work practice, bonus schemes and supervision (Ascher, 1987). Defending the proposals, the minister said that the act imposed fair competition, and that this market testing would ensure efficiency. The introduction of tendering was completed by 1991.

The latest stage in the process was the publication of a consultation paper – *Competing for Quality: Competition in the Provision of Local Services*, in November 1991. The government is able to extend the range of defined activities to white-collar services without resorting to primary legislation, but was required to do so to extend CCT to professional and technical services. CCT is seen as providing the cutting edge to the Citizen's Charter. The government also want to revise the framework of CCT to prevent 'anti- competitive behaviour', in fact by formalising internal markets and the client-contractor split. The tendering process is to be extended to:

- *manual services* – cleaning police buildings, maintaining police and fire service vehicles, home-to-school transport;
- *direct public services* – management of theatres and arts facilities, library support services, parking services;
- *contractor-related services* – architecture, engineering, property management;
- *corporate services* – corporate and administrative, legal, financial, personnel and computing.   (SLGIU, 1992)

The government has recognised that not all aspects of corporate services are suitable for CCT, when the work of officers is critical to the political process. However, the discipline of CCT is to be applied to all aspects of such services through the development of *internal trading accounts*, which break down each service into standard work components, identify standard unit costs, and define levels of work to be provided to internal clients.

So what has the *impact* of CCT been? First, it has been met with an attitude of hostility and resistance, since in the absence of a Scottish local New Right, it has few advocates outside government. Local authorities have shared their˜experiences in seminars and information through CCT Bulletins provided by COSLA. Indeed:

> The basic principle underlying the Convention's position is that services should be provided efficiently and effectively and that the best way to achieve this is normally to provide them through direct labour, i.e. by employees of the local authority . . . therefore the object is to preserve as many existing local authority jobs as possible by continuing to provide services on an in-house basis.   (COSLA, 1988)

The impact of these reforms in England and Wales has been analysed by Joe Painter (1991), who argues that a majority of authorities were committed to producing services in-house. In Scotland this was the predominant position, and collaborative defensive strategies were agreed with unions and employees. The result is that Scottish authorities have successfully retained services on an in-house basis (Stoker, 1988), winning 88 per cent of contracts, with a further 4 per cent being won by other authorities, compared with only 8 per cent by the private sector. In 51 per cent of cases, no competitive bid was received. As Black observed 'tendering in Scotland has resulted in fewer applications and fewer bids by private contractors: they have been less successful in winning contracts than elsewhere in Britain' (Black, 1993, p. 12).

This was not the outcome predicted in New Right rhetoric. Michael Forsyth (1980) argued that it would benefit ratepayers and business-men. On the first, the evidence is unconvincing, for the second, it has not produced the anticipated goldmine. The financial consequences of CCT are difficult to analyse. The impression given in most studies is of savings delivered. Black (1992) for example, found 'a general reduction in operating costs for the local services involved. The scale of savings is uncertain . . .' (p. 121). Accounts Commission reports identified potential savings in school cleaning and refuse collection. The problem is that 'savings' can and did arise in part because of the absence of specified standards of provision when delivered in-house. The introduction of CCT led in several cases to a lowering of standards, and hence costs. Secondly, it is also clear that 'savings' arose because of reducing the wages of already low-paid workers in the case of privatisation, or by reduced hours in the case of municipal provision. The final factor is the absence of an assessment of the 'costs' of CCT, in terms of monitoring, supervision, and administration. Although there has been no comprehensive study in Scotland, Szymanski and Wilkins (1992) found a deterioration of savings over time, as prices were increased second time around. It certainly hastened the rationalising of bonus shares which was already in process (Kerley and Wynn, 1990). These authors concluded that the claims of CCT enthusiasts in terms of financial savings are based on little evidence.

The benefits of CCT are clear enough. It hastened much-needed revision of work practices and ineffective bonus schemes. It has provided improved information systems on service standards by requiring costing of outputs, although this remains problematic in non-manual services. But it remains an unwanted reform, with strong objections to the *compulsory* nature of tendering.

CCT was presented as an economic reform. This ignores the question of the political values it raises. Many of the facets of contract compliance which have been removed were values which many Scots considered laudable. For example, the cutting of wages of low-income workers does not necessarily bring great cheer in a country characterised by high levels of poverty and benefit claimants. The requirement to provide employment opportunities for the disabled can be seen as a laudable public policy objective to overcome their inherent disadvantages in labour markets. In short, many of these aspects of contract compliance reflect social and political objectives, not pure economics. CCT in effect reflects a limited set of political values, not at all close to the hearts and minds of most Scots (Midwinter *et al.*, 1991).

Secondly, contract arrangements lack the organisational and policy making flexibilities of in-house provision, to shift staff to deal with unforeseen problems, or to give new priority in the light of changing circumstances. Thirdly, direct provision removes the element of uncertainty which is inherent in the private sector.

Finally, the contractual basis reduces the potential for democratic intervention, whether by local members or a change of political power. In the latter case, inherited contracts only frustrate the democratic process, as councils are legally committed by their predecessors. Practical problems and conflict will remain as long as the compulsory element remains. The attempt to clarify the client-contractor split is intended to reduce 'collusion' and promote competition. Black (1993) identifies several difficulties, including access of external contractors to council assets such as depots and vehicles; the tendering timetable; and adjustments to bids during tendering.

Promoting choice

The development of competition was intended to stimulate market efficiency in the supply of local services. The other side of the coin is the reform of the demand side. Pluralistic provision structures were the means to increase consumer choice. These ideas were initiated in the Thatcher years.

Parental choice

Parental choice became a cornerstone of Conservative education policy under the Parents Charter, and was enshrined in the legislation of 1981. This allowed parents to submit 'placing requests' for their child to be educated outside their designated catchment areas. More information on examination results was also promised as a means of enabling parents to make informed choices.

Ideology and practical administration are not easy bedfellows. Taken to extreme, the market model implied poor schools would improve or close, under the influence of parental sovereignty. The government recognised the administrative and financial constraints, by ensuring the policy was developed in the context of spending restraint in a period of declining pupil numbers and fiscal conservatism. Authorities could refuse requests on grounds of pupil numbers; additional costs of teaching and accommodation; and potential indiscipline.

The evidence of the impact of the legislation is fairly clear cut – it is a minority, mainly urban experience. In the 1980s, some 220 000 placing requests were made, and around 95 per cent were granted. That is, about 5 per cent of Scottish parents exercised these rights (Scottish Office, 1993a) and this ranges from around 14 per cent in Tayside, through 10 per cent in Glasgow, to 1–2 per cent in rural regional authorities. This pattern is not surprising, given the plethora of small schools and the distances between them in rural Scotland. There is also a much lower rate of request in Roman Catholic schools (Adler *et al.*, 1987). If the limited range of requests is a significant comment on the strategy, even more so are the reasons for requests. In the main: 'the concerns of parents tended to be pragmatic and pastoral in nature. Proximity and safety (on the one hand) and a concern with the happiness of their child were the dominant concerns' (Adler *et al.*, 1987, p. 310). These researchers concluded that parents were more influenced by social and psychological factors than educational ones. Although only a limited use was made by parents, it is clear that the exercise of choice has an impact on other children, if it results in 'undersubscribed' schools, and affects curriculum choices and educational opportunities. Parental choice can have effects beyond their own offspring.

A second area of reform was the replacement of school councils by school boards, and the subsequent provision for 'opting out' of local authority control. School councils were a 1970s expression of participatory democracy, and had a limited impact on educational issues, only one local authority – Strathclyde – allowing them to discuss curriculum matters. Enthusiasts for participation assume that this is what parents actually want, as the Main Report (Committee of Inquiry, 1986) showed that parents were keen to support educationalists in the interests of their children, rather than seeking direct involvement in ostensibly professional matters. The reform of school councils into school boards reflected a wider concern with school management, and the political objective of extending accountability to reflect the particular interests of parents and the local community in the provision of school education at local level. The legislation required the election of parent members by secret ballot, and although there are also teacher and co-opted members, parents form a majority. The functions allocated by the School Boards (Scotland) Act of 1988 are:

- to promote contact between the school, parents and the community and encourage the formation of a parent–teacher or parents association;
- to approve the headteacher's plans for use of the capitation allowance in books, stationery, and so on;
- to participate in the selection of senior promoted staff;
- to control the use of school promises outside school hours;
- to set occasional holidays during term time;
- to receive advice and reports from the headteacher and, in particular, an annual report which includes a report in the aggregated level of pupil attainment;

- to have any matter raised by the board considered by the headteacher and education authority;
- to receive information from the education authority about education in the area including statements about past and intended expenditure on schools.

Greater parental and community involvement would reduce local authority involvement in educational administration. The reservations expressed by local authorities over the declining influence of professionals or councillors have not proven well founded. Some 75 per cent of schools have boards, but there has been no wave of parental enthusiasm for involvement. They have tended to support the teachers *against* the politicians rather than regarding them as self-interested bureaucrats.

Munn (1992) regards the scope of board influence as limited to questioning and monitoring educational performance, not *decision-making*. Commenting on the pilot schemes of devolved financial management introduced in Dumfries and Galloway and Strathclyde Regions, she sees the headteacher as the real decision-maker. This sits easily with parents'

> general trust in the professional expertise of teachers and a belief that schools are doing a good job. So boards have not acted as thorns in the school's flesh; rather they have been harnessed to support schools and to put pressure on education authorities for more resources in schools.   (p. 147)

These same authorities will no doubt make the boards widely aware of the government-enforced expenditure constraints on themselves. In short, they are behaving like conventional pressure groups in the political system whose activities the New Right regard as undesirable! This collective orientation may help explain the very tepid response in Scotland to 'opting out', or 'self-governing' schools. After four years on the statute book, only one school has opted out of the local authority system. This is in marked contrast with the growth of opting out in England.

Market principles in education, as in other areas, embody principles of inequality in provision that run contrary to the fundamental goals of the post-war welfare state of free and equal access to education. The very notion of competition assumes that, although the government presents it as an extension of parental choice rather than as a source of inequality:

> Self-governing schools would be free to develop distinctive approaches in aspects of curriculum provision, in teaching methods and in the general ethos of the school. Self-government within the state sector would offer a real choice to parents. (Scottish Office Education Department, 1988)

This argument assumed that local board members would be more responsive to parental wishes than councillors would be. Yet there is no reason to believe that the majority of parents desire greater control over education in this sense – indeed, school boards have faced a shortage of candidates. The evidence over school boards is that parents desire a consultative and adviser role from them, not a governing role. Government reforms which run against the grain of such opinion, as with 'opting out', will be disappointed.

Housing policy

In *housing policy*, the Conservatives have shown a predisposition to owner-occupation and a disdain for the managerial competence of local authorities. They have sought to promote both home ownership and tenant choice.

The first development was the passage of the Tenants' Rights, etc. (Scotland) Act 1980, which provided for local authority tenants to purchase their houses with discounts and the right to a mortgage. In the subsequent decade, 24 per cent of municipal housing has been sold. In addition to the discounts, the government pushed up council rents by reducing Housing Support Grant and eliminating Rate Fund Contributions to the Housing Reserve Account. Whereas in 1979, *all* authorities received some subsidy, and rents accounted for 47 per cent of income, by 1991 half of all Scottish authorities received no subsidy, and rental income had risen to 95 per cent of housing budgets. The result of this process is known as 'residualisation', whereby municipal housing performs a welfare function for poor households, with reduced capacity to provide the more desirable type of housing:

In almost all authorities sales have been concentrated in semi-detached and terraced housing (89.5 per cent of all sales) particularly those built in the 1920s and since 1965. These houses represent the cream of the housing stock, and their sale substantially affects the image, in qualitative terms, of public sector housing. On the other hand, sales of flats and maisonettes which made up half the housing stock account for only 10.5 per cent of all sales.   (Alexander, D., 1985, p. 158)

In the absence of a new building programme, this clearly reduces the stock of desirable properties on offer, although most of these would not have become available for relet until the 1990s. This led MacLennan (1989) to conclude that council house sales have so far had little influence, positive or negative, on real housing problems. When seen as part of a broader package of policies, that view is perhaps optimistic. With a majority of tenants now in receipt of housing benefit, and the municipal housing stock declining in numbers and quality, the prospects of attaining more desirable properties has clearly been diminished for many Scots families. The sale of council houses – as with parental choice of school – can have negative effects for other citizens, both in reducing their choice, and in increasing the cost to them of maintaining the residual, poorer quality housing stock.

The Housing Scotland (Act) 1988 further advanced competition and choice in the housing market. It increased the roles of housing associations and private renting in the housing market, and reduced further the role of municipal housing authorities. This change envisaged local authorities as the 'strategic housing authorities' for their area – assessing need and ensuring it is met by other agencies. The Act also permits the transfer of local authority stock to other organisations, with the consent of a majority of their tenants.

The relevance of this choice is open to doubt, given the limitations of income of municipal tenants:

The conventional view of choice, that of consumers having a variety of options from which to pick, shoppers selecting breakfast cereals from supermarket shelves, does not operate within this context. For most council tenants, in opting to transfer their landlord, there will be but one choice on offer – a housing association or co-operative. They will not get to choose from a range of options.   (Robertson, 1990, p. 87)

Many of these organisations, and the new housing trusts, will be managed by staff whose background is in public sector housing management.

Social Work

In the 1990s, though the rhetoric of increasing choice through markets is still employed, there has been an increasing emphasis on managerial decentralisation and 'internal market' models. *Social work*, for example, has a long experience of operating a mixed economy of social care, with a heavy emphasis on the voluntary sector, particularly churches. In the 1980s, however, there has been an expansion of private provision (Table 4.1).

Table 4.1 *Ratio of municipal/'private'/voluntary premises in residential care*

Function	1980	1990
Local Authorities	65	54
Private	1	21
Voluntary	34	25
Total	100	100

Source: *SWSG Statistical Bulletin*, no CMC 1/1991.

The number of elderly residents in private residential care more than trebled from 924 in 1985 to·3224 in 1990. However, this change 'was a result of the unintended consequences of social security changes rather than a pro-active strategy for market provision or welfare pluralism' (Wistow *et al.*, 1992, p. 28). The public expenditure consequences of this growth for the UK as a whole has been substantial, rising from a negligible £10 million in 1979, to over £1000 million in the 1990s. Given its ideological predisposition against public spending, it is little wonder that a major revision of social care was initiated by the government.

Social work in Scotland developed in a piecemeal fashion, with separate welfare, children and probation departments. The common elements of social work practice led to their merger in social work departments in 1968, so that comprehensive social work departments would take on responsibility for the provision of supportive services to the proposed children's panels, together with a wide range of other duties that had previously been carried out separately by children's departments, welfare departments, public health departments and the probation service.   (English, 1988, p. 120).

These departments have a statutory duty to promote social welfare, although the scale of such provision is deemed to be a matter for local assessment of need. Social workers have a set of professional values which makes them sceptical of the value of market solutions in social work (Wistow *et al.*, 1992, p. 31). Their clients tend to be in acute social need, whether through problems of poverty, poor housing or longevity. In terms of child care, for example, the dominant political view of parental responsibility leaves them essentially in a role of residual welfare provision dealing with special needs (Cohen, 1991, p. 218). The privatisation strategy, with its emphasis on economic pricing, would not necessarily regard social work as fertile soil. The government therefore, chose to concentrate on the community care dimension and emphasise the enabling role of social work departments.

The development of community care itself has a longer pedigree, although its progress in a Scottish context has been limited, (Hunter and Wistow, 1988) in part because of professional commitment to institutional care, particularly in the NHS. In terms of both health and social care, Scotland enjoys high levels of funding (ibid., p. 94). The simple objective is to enable people to live as full and independent a life in the community as possible. In the case of the elderly, the home help service, meals-on-wheels and sheltered housing are principal instruments for achieving this, and the numbers receiving such services grew rapidly in the 1980s.

Pressures on public spending made the field an obvious target for review. However, the initiative came from a paper by the English Audit Commission (1984) which argued that the funding mechanisms and policy objectives were contradictory and unclear, and that the special income support arrangements applying to residents in private and voluntary sector houses constituted a 'perverse incentive' by promoting residential care at the expense of care in the community. Wistow *et al.* (1991) found a progressive redefinement of the social work role to emphasise social works responsibility for both creating a mixed economy and managing it more systematically since 1982. The Griffiths Report developed this further by advocating the purchasing role within a market place of competing providers, thus promoting choice and efficiency (Griffiths, 1988, pp. 1–3.4).

Scottish ministers agreed with the thrust of Griffiths's argument. The Scottish Secretary, Malcolm Rifkind, announced his position in a written parliamentary answer in July 1989:

> I have decided that local authorities in Scotland should be responsible for meeting the contribution from public funds towards the cost of the care of people in private and voluntary residential care and in nursing homes. They will in collaboration with health boards assess the care needs of individuals applying for such support and will reach a view on whether residential care is required or whether, in view of the primary objective of sustaining people in their own homes, a better outcome is possible by devising suitable individual packages of care.

The development of community care policy gave social work departments a lead role in the planning of service provision, in the 1989 White Paper *Caring for People*. Such departments, like housing and education departments, remain the major direct providers of service. They have now also become the major 'purchaser' of such services for the private and voluntary sector, with duties to:

- become responsible for assessing individual need, and design and secure delivery of relevant packages of care;
- produce and publish community care plans;
- promote the private and voluntary sectors;
- establish arm's length inspection units to monitor providers.

This was to be achieved by a new funding structure which eliminated the special arrangements and shifted all recipients to income support and housing benefit irrespective of their form of residency, except for residents in local authority houses who continue to be funded in the same way. The emphasis on 'planning' is of course in direct contradiction to 'market' concepts of choice which see the invisible hand at play in adjusting supply and demand.

The major change is the decentralisation of resource allocation within departments, on the GP fund holder model in the NHS:

> Under the White Paper on social care, a 'case manager' would be appointed for each client to construct a package of care for the client concerned, based on a predetermined budget. In making up the

package of care, the case manager would consider bids from competing provider organisations, including public, voluntary and private sector agencies.   (Le Grand, 1990, p. 4)

The care manager, as budget holder, becomes an important player in resource allocation. The choice of the consumer is limited by the resource constraints facing the budget manager, and supply constraints relative to their desired area and residence. The client still lacks effective purchasing powers.

Common *et al.* (1993) regard this model as a minimum level of market reform, and call it 'playing at shops'. The problem is that service-users are still dependent on the department to gain access to services provided by them. In short, the purchaser-provider split in practice is potentially only a superficial name change for a conventional management/professional relationship. It need not greatly enhance consumer choice, as

> [Even] if the purchaser has established a market in which there is a choice of supplier, this choice may not be made available to the service user. For example, when local authority social services departments contract with the voluntary or private sectors for the provision of community care, the person who needs the service may still be faced with no choice of provider. (Common *et al.*, 1993, p. 47)

The Act gives authorities a specific duty to undertake individual assessment of need, through consultation with the individual and relevant agencies. As the service remains publicly funded, with budgetary limitations, it is then the responsibility of social work authorities to design appropriate care packages within the resource constraints. Service delivery may be by the local authority, private or voluntary sector.

The White Paper set out the objectives of the reforms as follows:

- to promote the development of domiciliary, day and respite services to enable people to live in their own homes wherever feasible and sensible;
- to ensure that service providers make practical support for carers a high priority;
- to make proper assessment of need and good care management the cornerstone of high quality care;

- to promote the development of a flourishing independent sector alongside good quality public services;
- to clarify the responsibilities of agencies and so make it easier to hold them to account for their performance; and
- to secure better value for taxpayers money by introducing a new funding structure for social care. (*Caring for People*, 1.11)

The need for shared assessments and common goals for care groups was also emphasised by government, through placing agreements between local authorities and health boards. These would require strategic objectives and priorities, local assessments of needs, and monitoring of performance. Consultation with housing agencies would also be necessary. Evaluation of the practical impact of these reforms will only develop in the long term. The new planning, budgetary, assessment, delivery and monitoring systems are clearly experimental, with little empirical testing yet of practice elsewhere as the basis of comparison.

The big question

The extent to which planning and market principles can be combined is *the big question* hanging over the reforms. A recent paper produced for the Working Party on Local Government Finance neatly summarised the problem of unleashing private provision.

> The desire for objectivity . . . is particularly relevant in the field of independent sector residential care and nursing homes which have developed, particularly of late, not according to the needs of clients in any area but in accordance with commercial factors. Their development has been very much unplanned and uncontrolled.

This creates a problem for distributing the transferred resources from the DSS on the basis of relative need.

> Distribution on the basis of the present pattern of DSS expenditure within Scotland would put the new resources to the authorities with the stock of residential care and nursing homes. But this would perpetuate an unplanned approach to service provision which has no regard to the needs of those in the area. (LGFS (D) (92) 1 pp. 1 and 2)

However, moving immediately to a needs-based allocation would have caused financial problems for private residential care, as some homes were already operating with spare capacity. If authorities lost resources, so too would the providers, many of whom had been established reactively to the DSS arrangements, and constituted fairly major investments from individuals. Too great a loss of resources could result in closure, particularly in the rural areas of the Borders and Highlands, where needs-based assessments were 83 per cent and 104 per cent less than the pattern promoted through the DSS payments system. Problems will emerge when the transitional arrangements end and homes have to close to provide the necessary rationalisation. Indeed, some homes deliberately filled up their vacant beds prior to the change to maximise DSS payments, and thus further showed the needs basis of care. This has raised concerns in local government, and not only in social work circles:

> there seems to have been no attempt to estimate properly the costs of community care. The DSS resource which would otherwise have been provided to finance care through social security payments to people in residential nursing homes will transfer to local authorities, but no-one has made any assessment as to whether this will be adequate or not.   (Comely, 1990, para. 4)

This housing director went on to raise doubts about the adequacy of housing capital allocations in meeting such needs. A similar concern about the costs of community care was voiced by COSLA, who estimated that the additional infrastructure costs of implementation would be around £26 million, to establish the information and budgetary control system necessary to administer the system (COSLA, 1990).

Community care policy leaves key questions unanswerable at the moment. How extensive a choice will this model provide in practice? Will consumers be dependent upon available places and/or case managers? Will the policy be adequately resourced ? The argument for market principles is the capacity of markets to respond to demand, backed up by ability-to-pay. In the context of social care, increased demand for a particular form of care may not lead to increased 'production', through the absence of an effective price mechanism to regulate the process. Whether, in practice, the system will amount to anything more than the decentralisation of resource allocation within social work bureaucracies is questionable. It appears to be still a form of bureaucratic rationing with greater consumer consultation, with a slightly more diverse pattern of provision, than anything resembling a competitive market. Conflicting pressures are now at work:

> On the one hand there will be financial pressure for local authorities to cease using their own homes and buy places in private sector homes. On the other hand, there will now be effective cash limits on the expansion of commercial residential care; local authorities will be keen to negotiate cost-effective packages; and they may prefer to place clients in the voluntary sector rather than the commercial sector. (SLGIU, 1990, p. 15)

Professional concern over the purchaser-provider split exists because it places control of resources with the former, whether the latter may actually have the better understanding of client need. Quasi-markets in social work fall a long way short of markets in the private sector of the economy. The stress on the need for planning is in itself a recognition of the limits to markets which do not adjust in response to demand, but to open-ended public finance in the case of private provision, or politically determined budget limits in the case of public provision. The impact of this experiment in social care is still unclear.

In education, given the tepid public interest in self- governing schools, policy has focused on budgetary decentralisation through the devolved management of schools. Under this approach, education authorities will:

> [continue] to provide general support and advice to schools. They will also remain directly responsible for strategic decisions on the general provision of schools and school buildings and for other aspects of education provision which are sensibly provided at an education authority level, such as school transport, bursaries, re- cruitment advertising and incoming teacher training. They would also be responsible for the allocation of delegated budgets to schools. (Scottish Office, 1992)

The government's arguments for change can be summarised briefly. They are based on the principle that decisions affecting individual schools should wherever possible be taken at school level, and that parents and the local community should be involved. Devolved management will provide for greater flexibility; be responsible to local needs; reduce bureaucracy; provide greater accountability; and save money.

In sum, this will improve the 'quality' of the decision- making, and will enhance choice and staff morale. Education authorities will have a strategic, enabling role. Devolved budgets, with certain exceptions, will cover staff costs; furniture; fixtures and fittings; property-related costs; and supplies and services. At least 80 per cent of the non-exempt education expenditure should be devolved to head teachers. Such budgets should:

- take account of any minimum staffing standards set by the education authority – and be based on *actual costs* or *average costs*;
- allow head teachers to determine spending of a 'significant element' of *property-related* costs;
- distinguish between *books, materials and educational equipment* and *other supplies* and services.

The managerial approach advocated follows a pattern common to public services in the 1980s. There are, however, two major problems with the underlying assumptions. First, the *real* choice open to head teachers in devolved budgeting will be limited. In practical terms, most education authorities will work on an actual cost basis – as average costs were extremely problematic in England. Staffing costs vary with the age profile of teachers, not just school numbers. New resources for teaching staff will be determined at the centre of the authority, through its definition of minimum standards, and other policy decisions. Some flexibility through virement will occur, but with council budgets tightly capped, some disillusionment is inevitable.

Devolved management will have less impact in practice than the political rhetoric implies. The management reforms still require strategic vision and professional leadership at the centre of the authority. The problem with the market strategy is the almost naïve faith in reforming 'systems', and the assumption that competition and choice will of themselves improve the education service. Rather, this review suggests the market model has only a limited relevance to education management, and is in conflict with the need in public policy to manage the system as a whole.

Of the three major social services, it is only in housing that there are significant proposals to extend CCT in the 1990s. The advantages of such a change, however, remain at the level of abstract theory rather than concrete evidence. The government present this as a means of improving quality, efficiency and value-for-money, while promoting the enabling role. Managerial decentralisation is also advocated and the prospect of developing 'Next Step' type agencies in an internal market system. Managerial decentralisation will provide a better service and encourage competition (SOED, 1992).

This brought protest from local government, in the light of the government's own mixed evidence of cost and benefits, particularly as the alternatives are 'untried'. The paper lays little stress on the social and welfare dimension to housing management, and fails to acknowledge – again as with education – that decentralisation can increase bureaucracy and costs, as the management costs of housing associations show (COSLA, 1992). Given the government's philosophy, one would have expected support from tenants, yet the government was widely attacked for failing to consult with them in the first place. The reason for this is not difficult to understand: it is that tenants, like parents, have a less hostile view of municipal performance than Conservative politicians. Tenants have been reactive in the process, and have high levels of general satisfaction with their council housing (Miller, 1986).

As with education, there is no real evidence correlating quasi-markets with improving performance in substantive aspects of housing policy. Competition and choice will not tackle the growing problem of homelessness, dampness, or difficult-to-let properties, and changing tenure or landlord does not of itself alter the scope or mix of housing available:

> The crucial point is that tenure change cannot on its own improve housing conditions or satisfy need: only increased investment can do that. Increasing rates of owner-occupation merely redistributed housing resources, and the pattern of that redistribution is on the whole regressive.   (Alexander, D., 1985, p. 160)

There is no correlation between owner-occupation and housing quality. Nor is the pretext of 'choice' unsupported by the economic capacity to exercise it particularly meaningful. As with education, the reality of housing choice created by privatisation is both limited and achieved at the expense of others, in this case at the expense of the housing opportunity for low-income households in the community. Furthermore, it is not achieved without cost, and for no clearly *identifiable* gains in efficiency. Indeed, the availability of desirable, rented social housing is in decline.

Finally, as the government has recognised, the shift to the enabling role will take a long time to effect. With 700 000 homes still in municipal ownership, with sales in decline, and in the absence of any rush to transfer landlords, municipal provision will remain a dominant feature of Scotland's housing.

Constraints and contradictions of privatisation

The enabling authority model has emerged as the government's preferred instrument for imposing market discipline and business management techniques on local government. This derives from a theoretical critique of the inefficiency of municipally provided, publicly financed services in terms of both cost and responsiveness to customers. In essence, the Conservatives' concept of enabling is a much narrower and more economistic one than the community empowerment concept of the left (Gyford, 1991). It contains certain key emphases:

- on the benefits of ending monopoly service provision by local government and promoting competition;
- on the benefits of enhancing consumer choice within municipal services;
- on the benefits of adopting a tight managerialist model with clearly defined tasks, objectives and targets.

This new market discipline, however, falls far short of containing the properties of classical economic theory. In markets, competition between producers is determined by consumer sovereignty, exercising choice via the price mechanism, and consuming directly the goods exchanged for cash in the market. This creates a system of market accountability, which economic theory argues ensures efficiency. Although the limits of economic theory are widely recognised, the quasi- markets of the enabling authority approach still stand in stark contrast to the realities of imperfect competition in markets.

Under the enabling authority concept, there is limited competition. The extent to which dissatisfied consumers of municipal services can change their 'providers' is limited, and in many cases, access to the service is not delivered by a purchase, but still by bureaucratic resource allocation, whether to a rented house, or home for the elderly, or a place at school. The logic of markets is at odds with the logic of public provision for the collective benefit of the community.

In the quasi-market model, then, the practice falls short of market principles in key areas. The system of limited suppliers, financed by contract or earmarked budget, is a system which considers the wants of consumers, but may not yet reflect them. In essence, such contract relationships, whether through tendering or internal markets, constitute systems of managerial accountability, in which policy-making and service- delivery systems are separated. How effective this approach is as a model of municipal management must be open to doubt. Pollitt (1993) described it as 'neo-Taylorism', the rediscovery of scientific management from the early years of this century, and argues that

> its realism seems flawed by its resuscitation of the old Wilsonian politics/administration disharmony. That in practice there is usually no clear line between public 'missions' and the relation of means for their achievement has been repeatedly established in empirical studies. (p. 162)

If the enabling authority model is to be preferred to the conventional municipal provision model, then the case must be made clearly in terms of its impact in practice by empirical analysis, not by a theoretical critique of the inefficiency of the alternative, nor by reference to the more general benefits of market provision. In practice, as we have seen, there are a number of constraints and contradictions which raise substantial issues about its preferability, and moreover, its applicability.

The lack of competition in the major services is a major *market constraint* on the development of the enabling authority model. This has been tacitly recognised by the Conservatives, in their limiting CCT to services where existing private sector alternatives exist – in the construction, catering and cleaning industries, and in professional services such as law and accountancy. In mainstream services such as education and social work, the government has gone down the route of the much weaker internal market model of the NHS. Theoretically it is possible to see elements of policing contracted out, but in practice there could be political consequences of such a move in a service held in high public esteem. The result is that the share of revenue spending, even after the extension of CCT envisaged in 'Competing for Quality' will be *less than 10 per cent*.

Local authorities have *always* made use of the private sector in the delivery of services, but it has been on the basis of such activity forming an appropriate mechanism for a specific organisational need, not as a blanket policy based on as yet unsubstantiated assumptions about the benefits of competition. The theoretical critique on which CCT is based needs to be reconciled with the limited possibilities for market testing in practice. In Scotland, even more so than in England, it is still the case that 'councils are still major providers of housing, personal social services, schools and environmental services' (Travers, 1993).

There are also real constraints on *choice*. This weakness has been accurately analysed by Stewart and Walsh (1992), who see 'consumerism' as an inadequate basis for the complexities of public action, in which public organisations have to exercise coercive powers, of inspections and control over private actions. Under CCT, competition and consumer choice are controlled and lack the essential components of a competitive market. Under internal markets, the choice is bureaucratically managed, as we have seen in education, social work and housing. The absence of effective purchasing power restrains consumer choice and maintains bureaucratic resource allocation, albeit on a decentralised basis. As Allan Cochrane observed, the market model looks less like an assessment of what has happened and more like a picture of what some people would like to happen (Cochrane, 1991). Quasi-markets are poor substitutes for real markets in promoting consumer choice.

Finally, the development of privatisation policy is hampered by *organisational constraints* in what is essentially a hostile environment. The speed with which private contractors relinquished contracts in some areas is perhaps the most public evidence of this feature. There is a world of difference in supplying a service to an eager customer rather than to a reluctant purchaser looking for every opportunity to deprive you of your contract. Moreover, it is clear that within the terms if not the spirit of the legislation, authorities have gone to considerable lengths to maximise their potential to retain contracts or control internal markets. This organisational opposition is both political and professional, and the latter is perhaps of greater significance because of its permanence. One research study discovered that managers viewed these changes as politically imposed rather than organisationally necessary and beneficial, and often regarded them as inimical to public service values (Stewart and Walsh, 1992).

It is also the case that concern for the consumer can conflict with managing tight budgets and resource constraints. The appropriateness of the market model is questionable in such a context:

> Managing a service such as housing, social services or health care in which supply is limited by budget constraints does not require the same marketing skills as managing a business. More traditional skills of public administration, concerned with establishing firm rules and criteria, may be more appropriate. (Flynn, 1988, p. 28)

The business planning approach emphasises effective resource management, and problems of environmental and organisational complexity and uncertainty are played down. The model requires the clear specification of tasks, objectives and targets of classical management theory as a means of achieving bureaucratic accountability (Pollitt, 1993). One observer of the Scottish scene interprets the impact of such developments overoptimistically. Alan Alexander (1992) argues that the introduction of market discipline and business methods has been successful, and business planning and strategic management are increasingly part of the process of service design and delivery. A more realistic interpretation would be that the rhetoric of business management can be found, but its practical impact remains marginal.

The former head of the English Audit Commission set out seven criteria for a 'properly functioning system of local accountability'.

- *Clearly stated objectives for service outputs*
  Unless the aims of a particular service are generally understood and set out it is difficult to talk about success or failure, under or over achievement.
- *Identification of inputs*
  Without an assessment of the volume of resources devoted to an activity, it is difficult to evaluate the quality of stewardship of those resources.
- *Assessment of outputs*
  How well has the service performed against the specified objective ? If this assessment can be validated by some independent observer, so much the better.

- *Clarity of management responsibility*
  Who is responsible for which aspects of the service ? Do they – and, everyone else – know they are responsible?
- *Comparison of results*
  It should be possible to compare results from place to place. Without mechanisms of comparability – independently validated – the ratepayer or elector is ill-placed to judge performance.
- *Opinions*
  There should be some opportunity for those most directly concerned – the providers and the clients – to make their opinions felt, either directly or indirectly, regularly or intermittently.
- *Final sanction*
  Dismissal for poor performance.

(Davies, 1988, p. 58)

Davies' position is recognisable to students of public administration as the ghost of reformers past. The conceptual and measurement difficulties of such a model are ignored, the political dimension acknowledged but played down, and the mechanistic nature of the model unrecognised. The belief in comparison through performance measures, despite the acknowledged weaknesses of such an approach, is not surprising and is consistent with past reforms. Hood described it as the

cargo cult phenomenon – the endless rebirth, in spite of repeated failures, of the idea that substantive success can be gained by the practice of particular kinds of ritual . . . in a . . . recurring cycle of euphoria and disillusion in the promulgation of simplistic and stereotyped recipes for better public management. (Hood, 1991, p. 7)

Stewart and Ranson put it more simply: 'Public accountability will not be achieved by the reporting of simple performance measures' (1988, p. 19).

The privatisation strategy assumes that extending competition and choice is the way to improve efficiency. In practice, these can result in greater contradictory effects. Take for example, the issue of consumer choice – this can actually hamper efficiency. In 1993, the first successful 'opting-out' school was announced in Dornoch in Scotland, in which a small junior secondary school was allowed to opt-out following an application made after the local authority refused to upgrade it to a sixth form secondary school. Dornoch Academy has only 81 pupils and nine teachers. An alternative school is just ten miles away. The decision to opt out has divided the community and the teaching profession. The major objection to this exercise of parental choice is the wider public interest: it can have adverse effects for children at other schools in terms of educational quality, and it can add to costs and distort priorities. Capital approval for expansion will now come from government from within a finite resource cake. The exercise of private choices is difficult to reconcile with the public good (Macpherson, 1989). Consumer choice is by no means an efficient mechanism for developing public provision, indeed it can clearly be in contradiction to the efficient use of resources.

So too is the belief in competition. It comes into contradiction with the concern for efficiency in a number of ways. First, it requires the *extension* of bureaucracy to monitor the development and impact of the market, whether in terms of CCT or internal market reforms such as in social work. This is seldom included in calculations of the financial impact of these reforms. 'There is the possibility of extensive bureaucracy and organisational complexity since the trading relationship between client and contractor will require new and often elaborate accountability and control systems' (Stewart and Walsh, 1992, p. 513). Secondly, it brings into the provision of essential public services an element of *risk* which is undesirable. In one authority, for example, the successful contractor experienced difficulty in recruiting sufficient cleaning staff to carry out the contract, and the authority then had the cost of rehiring staff shortly after they had received redundancy payments. Thirdly, contractual obligations are more formal than service budgets, and have of essence a degree of organisational inflexibility which hinders efficiency and accountability. The democratic feedback on problems of service delivery which could be resolved through political intervention and perhaps policy reformulation is lost in the context of contract specification and three-year agreements. Finally, there is a clear contradiction between the purpose of these reforms – more effective control over the bureaucracy – - and their impact. Consumers of local services do not necessarily hold the same conspiratorial view of professionals as politicians, and in effect can become 'allies' of the professionals in arguments over resources. With tight cash constraints, this is a recipe for disillusionment, not efficiency. A seminar held by the government to promote opting-out of schools came up against just this contradiction. Rather than pursuing quality through choice, parents were seeking improvements which authorities could not deliver because of governmental constraints. Of those seeking self-governing status

> none intends to opt out in protest at their children's education. On the contrary, in each case they want more of what they have and praise what the regions have provided. Nor was anyone complaining that money is being wasted on bureaucracy . . .   (Fraser, 1993, p. 20)

In internal markets – whether through devolved management of schools, or case management in social work, tightly constrained rationing will be the order of the day. The scope for flexibility will be limited. The assumption of a better 'quality' of decision remains theoretical guesswork, in the absence of a clear market test for the outcome of the decisions. In some cases, this budgetary decentralisation can be seen as a restriction of choice driven by efficiency considerations, as in the transfer of DSS monies over residential care (Le Grand, 1990, p. 12).

Privatisation of local government remains an important element of Conservative thinking but its development is less extensive than its advocates assume – authorities are a long way from becoming enabling authorities. Indeed, CCT has had only a marginal impact on local government. Moreover, it is based on narrow economistic values, and ignores wider social and political values. It is therefore unlikely seriously to challenge the preference for conventional municipal provision in most Scottish councils. Abstract concepts of efficiency are not necessarily acceptable to the political process. Certainly, CCT has

> brought about some drastic changes in the attitudes and practices of direct labour organisations. Some aspects of direct labour organisation management in the past were difficult to defend and it is unlikely that any future Labour government would wish to restore them to their former protected status.   (Gunn, 1988, p. 22)

It has also certainly increased labour discipline and strengthened local management in negotiations (Dunleavy, 1986). However, not all politicians will see the reduction of staff conditions and incomes resulting from low-price costing as evidence of economic efficiency.

Such philosophical objections will prevent a consensus in favour of the enabling authority model from developing. More importantly, however, is the recognition that the necessary market conditions for its progress do not exist, and the use of quasi-markets in conditions of fiscal constraint results in contradictions which must be faced. It assumes a model of management and techniques of analysis which are less than adequate for municipal provision. The practice of the enabling authority model falls far short of the political rhetoric which underpins it.

5 Reshaping Local Authorities

The government's arguments

The Wheatley system was never fully accepted by Conservative Party activists, with discontent particularly acute in areas where power bases had been lost through subjugation in a larger regional authority – for example, in Ayr and Edinburgh. Stodart's review of 1982 was precluded from any proposals which would threaten the viability of either tier of local government. The result was a 'pressure simply ignored and left to flounder by Malcolm Rifkind' (Kerley, 1992, p. 27). However, Thatcher's fall and the Heseltine review in England gave a new impetus to reform. The new Scottish Secretary, Ian Lang, gave the first indication of a commitment to structural reform in an address to COSLA's annual conference in March 1991, in which he advocated the replacement of the two-tier system with a single-tier system, creating stronger, more effective authorities and clearer accountability, and said that the new financing arrangements post-community charge required capping, and local authorities would find accountability to the UK government more rigorous than local accountability.

This does seem a little inconsistent. Structural reform, including a review of the scope of local functions, is seen as a means of reducing bureaucracy and strengthening local accountability, and improving service delivery, whereas spending is seen to require accountability to the centre. Because authorities would conform to the 'enabling authority model', uniform size was unnecessary. The new system would be large enough to be properly resourced, but would reflect 'local allegiances'. Mr Lang promised a Green Paper, followed by wide consultation, so that reform could reflect the wishes of the people. The advocacy of local government reform was now taking place in the context of a wider commitment to 'take stock' of Scotland's governance. In response to the Scottish devolution issue in 1992, the government would examine the effectiveness of the Union, improving it but maintaining it. Ministers acknowledged that the Conservatives had been too abrasive with the Scots and needed a less partisan approach to the business of government. The need to tackle feelings of 'remoteness' was acknowledged.

The government's approach, however, despite the rhetoric of the Citizens Charter, still regarded electors narrowly as consumers. In line with the New Right critique of local government, power would be devolved to people, not political institutions, thereby 'enabling Scots to have more real decision-making power in their own hands' (Scottish Office, 1993b, p. 35). Local government was seen as central to this process:

> The Government's plans for the reform of local government are at the heart of their strategy to pass decision-making downwards. The new single-tier, all-purpose local authorities will be better able to promote effectively the interests of the area they represent. They will be able to identify more with their area. And they will be more accountable to the people who live there. In such, they will reflect the diversity of Scotland as a whole and revive the dynamism of local democracy. (p. 36)

The government's case for change was set out in a Consultation paper (Scottish Office, 1991b) which argued that the changes in both the role and the functions of local government since 1975 suggested a need for reform. The two-tier system was regarded as being 'not readily understood', leading to 'considerable confusion in the public mind' about responsibilities, which clouds accountability. Old allegiances to the 'old counties and county towns' remained, while some regional authorities were 'seen as too large and too remote from the local communities they serve'. There was a measure of duplication and waste, particularly over central administrative costs, and of delay and friction because of the two-tier system. Finally, the government's emphasis on consumer choice, competitive tendering, and private sector involvement, put the emphasis on the enabling role of local government rather than on direct service provision. This made the Wheatley Commission's concern with the operational advantages of large authorities less relevant.

A single-tier system was seen as the way forward. The existing system would provide the building blocks, but the new authorities should reflect local loyalties and allegiances. There was a strong emphasis on cost and value-for-money. What strikes the academic analyst, however, is the absence of any rigorous appraisal of the existing system. There is no coherent body of research evidence, but a reliance almost on anecdotes, rather than careful exposition and demonstration of a case for change. The case is treated as made, leaving only the form and scope to be determined. The parallels with the lack of analysis underpinning the introduction of the community charge spring readily to mind. The key arguments are made in a mere six pages of manuscript. A single-tier system would be simple to understand, devoid of waste, duplication and friction, and would increase the capacity of authorities to act as enablers, facilitating flexibility and the best use of scarce resources. So what is the evidence on these issues?

The research evidence

The notion that the Wheatley system has high bureaucratic costs is not new, it was commonly argued in the 1970s by ratepayers' groups and others. Empirical analysis suggests otherwise. Page's study for the Wheatley Commission found economies of scale in administration which

> supports the commonsense conclusion that administrative facilities can be deployed over an increased range of services and a higher volume of operational activity without a proportional increase in costs and with the advantageous use of specialists. (Page, C. S., 1969).

His work showed that the average proportion of total expenditure spent on administration in the small burghs examined was 21.6 per cent, as compared with 10.8 per cent in the large burghs, 2.3 per cent in the cities and 2.4 per cent in the counties.

A similar study of the present system reached similar conclusions. Utilising the statistical technique of regression analysis, E. Page and A. Midwinter (1981) found a negative correlation between district size and the proportion of the local budget spent on administration, and no relationship between the size of the region and its administrative costs. Again, this runs contrary to the conventional wisdom which assumes such costs are greater in the larger authorities. Whereas the average bureaucratic costs for regions are less than 3 per cent, in the districts the comparative figure is 8– 9 per cent. There is also evidence of higher administrative costs in small regions, with Borders (3.9 per cent), Orkney (5.1 per cent) and Western Isles (4.9 per cent) spending more than average (2.7 per cent). Shetland's performance (2.1 per cent) is skewed by its very high level of spending per se, although its administrative costs per capita in cash terms (£38) is well above the regional average (£21). Spending on administration is a small component of all local spending in Scotland, making scope for savings limited, but greater at a district level than at regional level.

We turn now to the question of duplication. The case on duplication is weak indeed. The government refers to the rationalisation achieved through the implementation of the Stodart Report, but points to duplication in terms of planning, industrial development, and urban research. The total spending in areas of overlap is 2.2 per cent of all expenditure. It seems a somewhat drastic step to reorganise the whole structure of local government to cope with overlap at the margins. Moreover, the degree of overlap is less than clear. Regional planners are concerned with strategic planning, whereas district planners concentrate on development control. These functions can hardly justify a wholesale restructuring of local government when the major services are all provided at the regional level. Such overlap that does exist between education, social work, police, fire, transport, water and sewerage is at the margins, and no evidence of major adverse impact exists in the public domain. If there is a concern with co-ordination, then why has there been promotion of a plethora of organisations in delivering social services, which makes implementation more difficult? Finally, some of the problems which do exist reflect differing *professional* values, and these will not disappear in a single-tier system (Young, R. G., 1983).

Turning to public confusion, there has been one major study of this issue, carried out for the Widdicombe Committee (Young, K., 1986). First, Young examined electors' capacity to name their regional or district council correctly. In both cases, 52 per cent did so. This is a stark contrast to England, where more can identify the smaller councils than the name of the county council. It is also a higher percentage than the 36 per cent of Scots who could name the Scottish Office correctly as the major government department in Scotland. Secondly, he examined understanding of the location of seven services, using four district and three regional services. These are set out in Table 5.1. In five of the seven services, a majority could correctly locate the service. Least knowledge was shown in terms of home helps and planning applications. We do not find this surprising, as both are used by only a minority of the community. Young concluded that though the scope of local government provision is fairly well understood, the structure of health administration was not, with 59 per cent of respondents identifying it as a local authority service; this error was most prevalent in Scotland.

Table 5.1 *Correct allocation of local government services in Scotland*

Service	% Correct
Schools	55
Housing	73
Street cleaning	73
Home helps	27
Rubbish collection	74
Planning applications	39
Fire service	57

Source: Derived from K. Young, 1986.

This does not suggest that the creation of a single-tier system will greatly enhance clarity and understanding, and hence accountability. Young's analysis showed that 42 per cent of Scots electors could correctly name their local councillor, and more than 69 per cent could name the party controlling both tiers of council. These statistics warrant the conclusion that there is a reasonable level of awareness of local government services and their locations, and that there is less confusion than the advocates of reform imagine. Finally, it is worth looking at satisfaction levels with local services, for dissatisfaction would provide good grounds for considering structural reform (see Table 5.2). In Scotland, high levels of satisfaction were recorded. Indeed, the low level of satisfaction with council housing reflects the views of people not actually living in council housing. More than half of council tenants were satisfied with their services.

Young's evidence, when compared with the Wheatley Research, shows broadly similar levels of understanding under both systems. The important question, however, is not over abstract issues of

Table 5.2 *Satisfaction with local services*

Service	% Satisfied
Schools	57
Council housing	41
Street cleaning	78
Rubbish collection	80
Fire service	76

Source: Derived from K. Young, 1986.

accountability, but whether this limited amount of confusion actually prevents citizens obtaining access to services, and there is no evidence that this is so. Indeed, both studies revealed citizens have a favourable disposition towards the services they receive, recording high levels of public satisfaction.

Thus one major study of public understanding of the present system shows that the system is well understood, and the government has singularly failed to produce any evidence to support its assertions about problems of confusion and accountability.

Finally, let us turn now to the question of the new enabling role of local authorities. In the Consultation Paper, the original Wheatley arguments for reform are seen to have less validity because of significant internal and external changes:

The creation of school boards, the option of self- governing status for schools, the promotion of home ownership and greater choice for tenants within the rented housing sector, the deregulation and privatisation of transport services, the co-operative attempts to tackle the problems of urban renewal, the impact of competitive tendering – all of these have had a major impact on local authority services. They have changed the way in which authorities discharge their statutory functions and the way in which they organise themselves administratively. The emphasis is now increasingly on the enabling role of local government, rather than on direct service provision. (para. 12)

This seemingly lengthy list of developments exaggerates the degree of change, for – despite the weight given to these changes – we have seen that direct service provision remains the norm in local government. Competitive tendering applies to only a small fraction of local government activity, and the present extension will not greatly alter that position. There is no evidence yet that it is a model which can be applied to mainstream service provision: the high spending services such as education, social work, police and fire. CCT is still at the margins of local government activity, even in housing.

The conclusion this brings for reform is clear enough. The arguments made by Wheatley, in terms of the capacity of large authorities for strategic choice and efficient service provision, are not undermined by such developments. Indeed, the Wheatley division of major social and infrastructure services at regional level, and community services at district level still seems defensible today. In the Stodart Report (1981), arguments for the transfer of major services from regions to districts were consistently rejected: in the case of roads, transfer to districts would cause complications where projects straddled district boundaries; water and sewerage required regional administration because the high capital investment demanded an authority with substantial resources; regionalisation had permitted increased operational efficiency and better deployment of specialist services in the case of police, fire, education and social work. As yet, the case against the regional tier is at best theoretical. The empirical evidence in support of the government's underlying assumptions is notable for its absence. Finally, it is not at all clear that 'more local' equates with 'more accountable'. The arguments for reform on democratic grounds are based on the view that small-scale, local government is more democratic and more sensitive to local needs. In a comprehensive review of the research evidence from Britain and America, Newton concluded that the democratic merits of small units of government have been exaggerated and romanticised, whereas their democratic deficiencies have been overlooked (Newton, 1977).

The government also argues that reform would lead to a more active public interest and electoral turnout. Elections are a central mechanism of political accountability. We can measure the health of local political systems in Scotland by using three variables:

• Percentage turnout (in contested seats)
• Percentage seats contested
• Number of candidates (measured as candidates per seat).

We do not, however, have data on numbers of candidates for the pre-1974 system. Despite the belief that large regions are remote from their electors, the average turnout in regional elections has been marginally higher (1 per cent) in the post-reorganisation period than it was in the Scottish local elections held in the 1960s. The district average for the post-reorganisation period is similar at 46 per cent. Secondly, however, there has been a remarkable increase in electoral competition. The parties have regarded the regions as the major political prizes in local government. In the post-reorganisation period 1974–88, the five elections produced an average 79 per cent of district seats contested, in contrast to an average 87 per cent for regions. These figures are a vast improvement over the old system in general, and the counties in particular: whereas the average percentage of seats contested in the 1960s was 65 per cent, the figure for the counties was a mere 25 per cent. *Democratic competition has clearly improved under the new system.* The full set of results are recorded in Table 5.3.

Table 5.3   *Electoral competition in local government*

Type of authority	Poll (%)	Contested (%)
1960s		
Cities	38	96
Large burghs	43	86
Small burghs	49	56
Counties	56	26
Districts	55	16
1974 onwards		
Regions	46	87
Districts	46	79

Regional elections also consistently record a higher degree of electoral competition. The average number of candidates per ward was consistently *higher* in each election for regions, with an average of 2.88 candidates per ward, compared with 2.39 individuals per ward in district elections. Moreover, the differential increased over the period. The ratio of candidates per seat grew by 17.9 per cent in district seats, but by 30.7 per cent in regions. Parties and candidates had greater interest in regional elections.

Finally, we would also note that, despite the fact that in England the old counties persisted as shire counties in many cases, turnout in the 1970s was consistently higher in Scottish regions than English counties, at 48 per cent compared with 42 per cent. Overall, there is no evidence that regionalisation inhibits democratic participation. Contrary to the prevailing orthodoxy, Scottish regions compare favourably with districts and the shire counties.

The arguments reviewed

The government regarded the move to a single-tier system as reflecting a wider political consensus between the parties (McVicar *et al.*, 1994). The Liberals and the Scottish National Party have consistently favoured a single-tier local government system with strategic functions transferred to a Scottish parliament. Several of the government's arguments about remoteness, waste and confusion can be found in these parties' policy statements of the 1970s. Labour, like the Conservatives, came late to the notion of single-tier local government. By the late 1980s, it was concerned to disarm criticisms of its proposals for a Scottish Parliament, by reducing overgovernment through shifting to a single-tier local authorities. So by 1991, though all parties favoured single-tier local government, only the Conservatives did so *without* an accompanying programme of constitutional reform. The new political wisdom was that unitary authorities would enhance democracy and efficiency. When the government undertook consultation on the principle of change, the other parties opposed change in the absence of a Scottish parliament. But what of the wider public?

Some 470 submissions were made to the Scottish Office in response to the Green Paper; excluding local authorities, the number of responses was 393. Of those, some 26 per cent came from community councils, and 18 per cent from political parties. As one analysis of the responses revealed, *only* a majority of Conservative Party representatives supported the broad proposals. About one-third of respondents were critical of 'the case' for change, and only about the same figure supported a single-tier system in principle. Only 15 per cent of respondents felt local government was too remote, only 10 per cent favoured 'enabling' authorities, and only 8 per cent favoured the removal of powers from local government (McCrone *et al.*, 1992). Strong support for the government's agenda came from the Scottish Conservative and Unionist Association Local Government Review Committee, which adopted a more radical position:

> Local government reform should be firmly placed in the context of the policy trends of the last 12 years. To that extent the fundamental principles are those of empowering citizens, devolving power and responsibility to individuals, and providing for the efficient delivery of the important public services presently undertaken in local authorities. The committee endorses the vision of local authorities as enabling bodies securing the provision of public services by third parties whether they be private contractors or public agencies rather than as major service providers in their own right. (pp. 1–2)

This committee went on to argue for area education boards independent of local authorities and with membership made up from higher education and the business community. The local authority role in housing should cease; contracting out in social work should expand; strategic planning, trunk roads and A roads should become central government responsibilities; water and sewerage should be privatised; and police and fire should be funded by central government through advisory boards. In short, local government should be reduced in scope to less than existing districts. Like the Green Paper, this case is simply asserted, and the benefits of such change are treated as self-evident rather than demonstrated. The loss of democratic control this would entail is simply ignored.

Although critical of the government's lack of a case for change, Alan Alexander (1992) remains committed to the concept of a single-tier system. He argues that the fragmentation of service delivery creates uncertain lines of accountability. Alexander believes a sound case for a single-tier system exists, if not that made by government. However, he is supportive of the notion that large regions are remote, inaccessible and unaccountable. Although he does not provide any explanation why, he argues that

> Local government ought to be about the government of communities as well as about the effective delivery of services and there is a cogent argument which says that there is a point at which the creation of authorities that are big enough to improve service efficiency and to

facilitate redistribution acts against the notion of community government.   (Alexander, A., 1992, p. 59)

Regrettably, these elastic concepts of 'size' and 'community government' are left undeveloped, yet they are central to Alexander's
argument. We are left with the unhelpful notion that there is a point
where efficiency and democracy collide, but no way of knowing how to
define it. Secondly, Alexander falls for the government's argument
about the scale of change. He even talks of 'the demise of the providing
council'. This may be true of districts, but it is not even close to
capturing the working of regional authorities. However, with no
explanation why, he then goes on to conclude that this change makes
single-tier local government desirable. He provides *no reason* why this
should lead to a predisposition in favour of unitary local government.
In short, Alexander's case too remains at the level of theoretical
assertion.

By contrast, referring to reform in Wales, Boyne (1992) argues that it
hardly seems plausible that the 'complex' notion that counties provide
education while districts provide housing is beyond the intellectual
capacity of the electorate. The real test is whether single-tier authorities
will be more responsive to needs. For Boyne, the answer is clear
enough:

> It is unlikely that a single-tier system will provide policies that are
> better matched to electoral preferences. The number of councillors
> per elector will be reduced. Thus the weight of elected representatives
> in local government decisions will decline. In addition, the direct
> electoral impact of voters will be reduced. In the present system the
> public can vote separately at the county and district levels. Separate
> judgements can be passed on county and district performance and on
> the packages of services that each term provides. In a unitary system,
> electors will have only one vote to cast across the whole range of
> services.   (p. 2)

Boyne goes on to argue that the problems of co-ordination which result
from geographical interests rather than institutional ones will continue,
perhaps driven out of the public arena into group decision-making, and
professional conflicts will not be solved. Finally he argues that there is
empirical evidence that unitary authorities tend to be more expensive
(Ostrom, 1983; Schneider, 1986).

Arguments from a community perspective in favour of a 'multi-tiered' system have been made by John Stewart.

> Two-tier or the multi-tiered structure found in Europe give recognition to those widening circles of communities, going from the commune which can be based on a small town, through the wider areas equivalent to the county, to a region level, each grounded in a different sense of community – The case for a two-tier system is that both community and functions operate at different levels.   (Stewart, J., 1993, p. 9)

The first test of public perceptions of the government's proposals are in a System Three Survey carried out in September 1991. This showed 49 per cent of Scots favouring the status quo, whereas 37 per cent favoured a shift to a single-tier system.

A second consultation paper was published in 1992 (Scottish Office, 1992). 'Shaping the New Councils' sets out four possible systems, although stressing that the final decision would involve combinations of these. These were:

- *A 15-unit structure* – which basically retained all existing regional and islands councils except Strathclyde, which would be broken up into four units;
- *A 24-unit structure* – which subdivided all regions apart from Borders, Dumfries and Galloway, and Fife;
- *A 35-unit structure* – based mainly on existing districts or combinations of them;
- *A 51-unit structure* – with 34 existing districts, some combinations, and some new areas, such as Irvine, Paisley and Glenrothes.

These authorities ranged in size as shown in Table 5.4.

Table 5.4   *Range of population size of optional authorities*

Structure	Smallest unit	Largest unit
15-unit	103 500	927 700
24-unit	84 480	689 210
35-unit	49 440	689 210
51-unit	45 100	689 210

Source: *Shaping the New Councils*, pp. 80–7.

This document argued that there was now a general recognition that many services are better delivered by private businesses, and thus the need for very large authorities has been reduced. Support for a single-tier system had been received from a range of interests. Yet the government highlighted the need for efficiency, and recognised the problems this would cause for small authorities. The solution was to be joint arrangements for specialist services, which was regarded as unproblematic. The government had commissioned a report from consultants Touche Ross as to the likely costs of reform. This led to the conclusion that reform would produce long-term savings. The 15-unit option would save £192m. per year, whereas the 51-unit option would *add* £58m. to costs. Transitional costs would range from £185m. to £249m. over the first six years, leading to net savings of between £80m. and £100m. per annum. These conclusions were quickly welcomed by the Secretary of State:

> The Report makes a valuable contribution to the consultation process. The figures in the report are encouraging. They show how wide of the mark were all the speculative claims about costs which have been made recently and show that a single-tier structure can cost local taxpayers much less than the present two-tier system. It is, quite simply, not the case that this exercise is unaffordable. I believe in fact that we cannot afford not to reform local government. The Touche Ross study shows that the inevitable transitional costs will be recouped quickly by the savings which arise from moving to a single-tier system and that thereafter, there are substantial savings to be made.   (Scottish Office Press Release, 12 October 1992)

In fact, the consultants' figures were quickly challenged and weaknesses admitted. We shall examine this issue more closely in the next section. The interesting point is not the 'accuracy' of the figures, but the trend identified, which shows that savings arise when the small districts are abolished, *not* the regions. This is exactly the point we made earlier. If there is a case for reform, it cannot rest on myths about the high costs of large authorities. Moreover, it is clear that costs will rise with the number of authorities established. 'Shaping the New Councils' also included comment on the service implications of reform. In all but the 15-unit structure, more extensive use of joint arrangements will be necessary. Again, this has implications for service provision. We shall return to this issue in the third section of this chapter.

The White Paper finally emerged in July 1993. It proposed the creation of 28 new authorities, ranging in population size from 20 000 to 620 000. Police and fire services would remain organised in eight units, managed mainly by joint boards; water and sewerage would remain in the public sector, in three new public water authorities; and aspects of roads and the reporters' service would become central government responsibilities. Joint arrangements might be needed for aspects of education, social work, and structure planning. The picture that this portrays is of a potentially more complex, more fragmented structure of government.

Moreover, the government went on to create very small councils in Conservative strongholds, such as Eastwood, Stirling, and Berwickshire and East Lothian. Such authorities are only defensible in terms of political logic. Political objectives were raised in Conservative submissions to the consultation process, urging the government to maximise their political advantage (McCrone *et al.*, 1992). As Boyne *et al.* note, the efficiency arguments being deployed by advisers in favour of larger authorities came up against the anti-bureaucratic predisposition and partisan self-interests of influential Conservatives (Boyne *et al.*, 1994).

The White Paper, however, did not go nearly as far as the Thatcherite right had hoped. There has not been the wholesale emasculation of local government sought by the Adam Smith Institute or the SCUA Review Group, and water has not been privatised. We do not have a plethora of small, powerless authorities and most of the authorities are defensible in terms of socio-economic geography. The key question is, will it bring improvement?

The costs of reform

The government's argument is that the two-tier system inevitably results in duplication and waste through the need for central bureaucratic systems in each tier, and through the exercise of concurrent functions, whereas a single-tier system would remove these obstacles, facilitate flexible responses, and allow best use to be made of scarce financial and human resources. We recorded previously our scepticism at the validity of these assumptions. Bureaucratic costs by definition form only a minor part of local expenditure, and the *volume* of administrative work generated by service activities is unlikely to change greatly, as only those services removed from local authority costs offer the potential for anything other than *minor* financial savings.

It is important, therefore, to examine critically the evidence that does exist in terms of the costs of bureaucracy and the efficiency of service provision. To this end, the government commissioned a report from Touche Ross (1992) to examine these issues. Its remit was to develop methodologies for evaluating both the transitional and long-term costs of change; and cost up to four options for single-tier authorities. The study operated within set parameters, namely that:

- all existing functions should be assumed to remain with local authorities;
- the quantity and quality of services should be assumed to remain unchanged;
- no changes in management practices should be assumed (for example, from direct service to enabling authorities).

Touche Ross began with a sample survey of authorities from which it extrapolated costs for the whole system and developed organisational structures for the differing authorities contained in the recent consultation paper. They also calculated transitional costs, and from these made predictions about the costs of shifting to the alternative systems. However:

> The survey and financial modelling considered only those areas which were, therefore, likely to change. In the main, these were central support and corporate services, the management and administration of services and the provision of certain specialist expertise. Direct operational service costs were excluded, as the same quantity and quality of service was assumed. (p. 3)

From this, the report calculated the Ongoing Annual Savings as shown in Table 5.5. The report concluded that the 51-unit option would incur additional costs on an ongoing basis. It is not estimated to produce any savings in management and administration costs. The predicted savings from the other three structures result from the *merging of district services and from the removal of duplication.*

Table 5.5 *Predicted costs/savings of reform*

Map	No. of units	Annual costs/savings (£m)	% of current spending
1	15	−192	−2.6
2	24	−120	−1.6
3	35	−55	−0.7
4	51	+58	+0.8

Source: Touche Ross Report (1992) p. 4.

There are, however, a number of problems with the report which make it less than useful as a basis for reaching judgements about options. First, its calculation of transitional costs has been heavily criticised as an underestimate (COSLA, 1993). Secondly, there are problems of classification in some services – such as planning and economic development, libraries and social work – arising because some operational staff were included in the management/administrative category. This problem arose because the decision as to *whom to include* was made on salary grounds, which led to quantity surveyors, tourist officers, librarians and social workers being included, with the result that the base costs of these three services are overstated, making the prediction meaningless: the current management and administrative costs of planning and economic development appear to be greater than the whole of the service budget; the library estimate is roughly 20 per cent of actual library spending; and the social work estimate is £218m. compared with the actual costs of social work administration of around £40m. (Response of the Association of Directors of Social Work to the Consultation Paper, 1992). This means that the scale of savings for the various estimates is in need of revision.

Secondly, there are questions over the assessment of transitional costs. COSLA argued that:

- the potential costs of early retirement and redundancy have been significantly understated;
- the potential costs of relocation and recruitment were calculated by an inappropriate methodology;
- the costs of planning change have been underestimated;
- the costs of setting up Residuary Bodies are based on inadequate research; and

- the consultants failure to recognise that each unitary authority would wish to develop its own IT strategy at the earliest possible date and that there would be consequent greater cost the higher the number of authorities.   (COSLA, 1993)

Thirdly, there are problems with the assumption that operational costs should be excluded, and the same quantity and quality of service assumed. This assumes that functional efficiency does not vary with the size of the authority, although this was a central assumption of the Wheatley Report. Indeed, Touche Ross excluded the major regional services of police, fire, water and sewerage from their analysis, as these services 'could not effectively be delivered to areas smaller than those defined by the current boundaries' (p. 6). Analysing the link between size and efficiency is complex, and studies in the 1960s and 1970s looked for statistical evidence of economies of scale with increased size through regression analysis. This is not a very convincing way of undertaking the analysis. Newton's comprehensive review of these studies shows that the dependent variable used tended to be spending per capita, which, given the considerable degree of policy discretion open to local authorities in aspects of education, housing, social services, leisure and recreation and libraries, led to the absence of statistical evidence in support of the proposition. The economies of scale argument, however, refers to unit costs. It is that larger authorities show greater flexibility in managing resources, and greater advantages in purchasing than smaller ones. It does not necessarily mean they will spend more in *total*, as that will reflect political decisions about levels of service. Only in the case of administration is there evidence of economies of scale. This is entirely consistent with the point just made, as we would not expect politicians to want to spend more on bureaucracy in the way we would expect them to on service provision.

There are also problems with the technique used, which assumes that the influence of size is a general one held consistently through all sizes of authorities. It may be that the impact of size is found in *very big* or *very small* authorities, rather than in a linear relationship. In short, both the dependent variable and the statistical technique used are of questionable relevance to the analysis. Moreover, geography also has to be taken into account – for example, the demands of a compact urban population of 250 000 will be very different from those of a remote rural authority of the same size.

In the Scottish context, there is a mix of small remote rural regions, intermediate regions, and urban regions. These are likely in many services to have to incur *core operational costs* in service provision, such as police communication systems; major vehicles; snow clearance vehicles and equipment in roads; information and reference networks in public libraries; residential care facilities with organisational 'slack' in social work. Larger authorities will have more flexibility in *managing staff time*, and they will also be able to negotiate favourable *purchasing* agreements.

If efficiency analysis cannot be conducted in terms of simple per capita spending, what indicators can we use? One way of exploring the issue is through analysis of manpower levels in services which are not the focus of partisan political disagreement. Newton's (1981) study showed that Labour controlled councils tended to spend and provide more on 'highly politicised services such as education, housing and personal services'. However, there is no evidence of political control having been influential in infrastructure services or administration, so we can look for evidence of economies of scale by comparing spending in these services.

The results are shown in Table 5.6. In the four 'apolitical' services, all three small regions consistently spend above average. In the intermediate authorities, the three authorities spend above average in three cases out of four. In the urban authorities Lothian and Strathclyde, the two largest authorities, consistently spend below average, whereas the other (Central) is below on water and drainage, but above on roads and administration. In the 'politicised' services, no such clear pattern emerges. The small authorities are below average on social work and education (excluding Highland), the intermediate authorities are above average in each, while the urban authorities are below average in education and above average in social work. However, in education, central government takes a greater interest in minimum standards, whereas in social work, standards of care reflect local discretion. The comparison, however, shows below average costs in most services in the larger authorities, and particularly in those services of low political salience. Lothian and Strathclyde, the two largest authorities (0.7 and 2.4 millions respectively), benefit from their compact population geography, and have low costs of service provision. *It seems highly improbable that they could be broken up into smaller authorities without some loss of efficiency and consequently higher costs.*

104

Table 5.6 Spending on key services in Scottish Regions/Islands 1992–3 (£ per capita)

Authority	Education	Roads	Social work	Sewers and drains	Transport	Concessionary fares	Total	Population
Borders	442	88	114	16	8	2	1012	103 500
Central	454	50	127	9	6	5	935	272,100
Dumfries	464	71	113	13	10	4	1000	148 400
Fife	473	57	120	3	5	14	971	345 900
Grampian	442	52	112	7	3	7	912	506 100
Highland	511	154	97	8	6	2	1152	204 300
Lothian	409	40	142	6	5	8	941	749 600
Strathclyde	448	43	129	7	18	7	967	2 306 000
Tayside	447	63	136	6	7	12	970	394 000
Orkney	665	154	168	4	130	0	1592	19 570
Shetland	908	233	246	20	183	3	1856	22 270
Western Isles	739	158	170	3	36	2	1723	30 660
Scotland	451	54	128	7	13	7	976	

The cost implications of local government reform can be summarised briefly. First, the reforms will *not* generate major savings, and may actually add to costs. Secondly, the scope for savings *decreases* with the number of authorities established, as the larger, more efficient regions are dismantled. Thirdly, the scale of savings suggested by the Scottish Office is a mere guesstimate, reliant on hypothetical management structures based on the consultants' judgement.

In a letter to Tam Dalyell MP, the Scottish Secretary Ian Lang has modified his claim that 'substantial savings' would occur, to an assertion that the new system would be no more expensive to operate than the present system (April, 1993). The reality is that the estimates of the costs of reform are based on financial modelling, which in turn depends on the validity of its assumptions. We have shown that these are contentious. The real costs will result from political and managerial decisions of the new authorities, not consultants' estimates. The financial case for reform has not been made.

The illusion of accountability

The final theme of the reform agenda that needs consideration is that of accountability. The government's argument is that single-tier councils will remove the blurring of accountability and provide a clarity of responsibility and a greater sense of local identity. We have already shown the arguments about community understanding have little empirical support and that community identity is an elusive concept. The key issue, therefore, is simply whether a clarity of responsibility is on the cards.

The real obstacle to clarity of responsibility is the inability of small administrative councils to provide efficiently the full range of local government services. These arguments are similar to those made for the abolition of the metropolitan counties in England, as Leach *et al.* (1992) noted. 'It was presented as a measure for removing an unnecessary and superfluous tier of local government, . . . the term used by the government – streamlining – implied marginal change . . .' (p. 1). This research team went on to conclude:

joint action for anything other than a very limited range of services should be seen as an additional (indirectly elected) tier of local government which actually undermines, in a fundamental sense,

the 'unitary authority' principle. It raises major issues about processes of resource allocation, public comprehensibility and, in
particular, public accountability.   (p. 5)

The government appears to regard the necessity for joint boards as an
unwelcome but not insurmountable 'technical' problem, not one of
accountability. In a euphemistic tone, 'Shaping the New Councils'
observes

> under some of the possible structures, particularly those involving
> relatively small local authorities, it would be necessary for autho-
> rities to co-operate or act jointly in order to ensure the provision of
> the more specialist services. This need not however mean that an
> individual authority would relinquish control or responsibility for
> the provision of its service. The government are determined that an
> important aspect of the new single-tier authorities should be clear
> lines of accountability between local people and those they have
> elected to represent them. There is nothing new in local authorities
> combining to provide services: various arrangements already exist in
> the current system ranging from joint boards for police and fire to
> the use by smaller authorities of specialist facilities which are
> provided only by the larger authorities.   (p. 8)

The use of joint arrangements would *increase* with any of the options
on offer, even if it is more limited in the 15-unit option. This would
require at least additional joint boards for police, fire, water and
sewerage, because of the dismantling of Strathclyde Region. These
services amounted to over £800m. of local expenditure in the Region in
1992–93, compared to around £140m. spent through joint boards in
Scotland at the moment. The frequency of joint arrangements increases
greatly with the number of councils, whether through complete joint
provision for the aforementioned services, or for specialist aspects of
provision in education, social work, roads, public transport, and
libraries. How do such arrangements work?
  There are three main options for developing joint arrangements over
service provision. These are:

- *Joint boards* – legally constituted bodies as part of statutory
  provision of services by two or more councils; their membership,
  financing and management is subject to a Scheme of Administration

approved by the Secretary of State. At the moment these exist in police, fire and valuation services in parts of Scotland.

- *Joint committees* Under the 1973 Act local authorities may agree joint working arrangements through a joint committee, of which the only existing example is for libraries and museums in the north-east of Scotland.
- *Contract model* – whereby smaller authorities enter into a contractual arrangement with a larger authority for the provision of a specialist service, in the same way they would contract with a private company. At the moment, such practices occur for the secure accommodation of children in social work, or cross-boundary transfers of school pupils in education.

When we examine existing practice, however, joint arrangements look like cumbersome mechanisms of provision, and poor mechanisms of public accountability. In Borders Region, for example, the smaller partner's disillusionment with the functioning of the joint police board led to it requesting the Secretary of State to constitute a separate force after police services in the area were reduced when Lothian had its spending capped. This sort of situation occurs because of the practice of allocating an 'assessed need' figure for joint boards services to each authority in the calculation of the authority's Grant Aided Expenditure (GAE) – the Scottish equivalent of Standard Spending Assessments – which then becomes a benchmark for capping controls. In short, this means an individual authority is 'assessed' to have control over its expenditure on services which are in effect the legal responsibility of the joint board.

Joint boards

A good example of the lack of accountability in joint boards arises in the Highlands and Islands, where persistent problems of joint board financing occur, causing budgetary problems for the constituent authorities. One of the participants, Highland Region, has been in regular correspondence with the Scottish Office over this matter, and made the point forcibly in their submission over local government reform. They showed that boards are separate legal entities, and that 'members' are not accountable to their constituent authorities, let alone the public. Unlike all mainstream services, the majority of elected

members have no input into the affairs of the joint board through the
full council. Thus:

> This constitutional situation, in our experience, creates difficulties in
> terms of expenditure when Joint Boards follow expenditure policies
> which are different from those of constituent authorities. With
> modern day financial controls, such as capping, the requisitioning
> powers of the Joint Boards can place a constituent authority into a
> position of being capped, yet that constituent authority has no direct
> powers of control over that situation. This in turn may require
> reductions in expenditure by the constituent authority in services for
> which they do exercise a direct control, in order to avoid capping.
> This is clearly a constitutionally anomalous situation which detracts
> substantially from the notion of direct local accountability.   (High-
> land Region – Response to Consultation Paper)

It is clear, therefore, that when joint boards are necessary to deliver
economies of scale, the result is *weaker* accountability.

Joint committees

Joint committees are not likely to be widely developed in the new
structure. The existing single example functions efficiently because of
the non-partisan political system. Joint committees will be less
amenable to political control and policy co-ordination, and thus less
likely to be attractive to local politicians, particularly in urban areas
where party politics is a common feature of local government.

The contract model

In theory, this assumes a model of accountability based on competitive
tendering, where authorities *specify* the service required, and a private
contractor provides it for a fee. This is *not* how inter-authority
contracts work at the moment, rather the smaller authority 'buys in' to
an established service whose policy has been determined by the large
authority. In selling spare places, there is a real incentive to the selling
authority which would not exist if it had to tailor the service to the
demands of the purchaser.

Authorities' willingness to engage in such joint arrangements will
clearly be hampered by the political bitterness engendered through the

government's readiness in the new structure to protect its own political power-bases whatever the rationale of socio-economic geography. Political considerations over the Wheatley map were more pronounced in drawing district boundaries. Regional authorities do not reflect such issues.

In determining the new power structure, it is clear that the interests of the Conservative Party were paramount considerations. It is noticeable that, despite the claimed loyalties to old counties, few such counties have been recreated. Rather they have been divided, to deliver politically acceptable structures such as East Renfrewshire, East Dunbartonshire, South Ayrshire and Stirling.

Of course, it is only fair to record that the present structure of local government does not fully reflect the Conservative electoral performance, and over-rewards Labour because of the scale of the regions. Nevertheless, with the creation of greater Eastwood (East Renfrewshire); the survival of Stirling; and the abortive attempt to enlarge Berwickshire, it is difficult to see *any other logic* than partisan interest in the government's plans. So though Stirling district's leaders may talk at the present of reaching contractual arrangements with other councils, this could be politically impossible. Local authorities are political institutions, not businesses, and political factors will be important ones. In practice, the contract model will have only limited practical application. The extension of joint boards for police and fire, the new water and sewerage authorities, the removal of certain other functions to the centre, and the need for joint arrangements in aspects of education and social work, represent a fragmentation of democratic accountability rather than its clarification, and a reduction of democratic control.

6   Defending Local Government in Practice and Theory

Beyond the radical rhetoric

In the 1990s, the Conservative government presented a bold vision of radical reform in local government, achieved through financial controls, market discipline and structural change. Its detractors have argued that it is centralising power (Jones, 1992; Crouch and Maynard 1989), but its defenders see it as decentralising power to the citizen (Pirie 1988; Bulpitt 1989). The essence of the Conservative defence to this charge of creating a new centralism is straightforward:

> In changing the ways in which things have been done for decades, we are predictably accused of attacking local government. I emphatically reject that charge. Certainly local government's powers in certain respects will be limited, but they will be in practice not by the government but by local people.   (Ridley, 1988)

This is consistent with the presentation of the issue and their response to it by Thatcherites. Ridley saw the government as a radical one which was not prepared to rubber-stamp time- honoured policies that in his view led to Britain's decline. Firm government, with clear convictions and objectives, was at the head of this new approach to local government.

Bulpitt (1989) sees the government's policies towards local government as reflecting the view that the role of the state and public spending and taxation needed to be rolled back, and thus local authorities needed to be controlled in the interests of macro-economic management. Later, attention shifted to the supply side of the economy, and sought greater efficiency through the 'enabling authority' concept. This is simply: 'a more coherent version of what Michael Heseltine and Tom

King were trying to put over in the early 1980s. The strategy looks radical . . .' (p. 73). Other commentators agree with this interpretation of developments: Cochrane (1993) argues that there is widespread agreement that the position of local government within the British state system has changed significantly since the 1970s; Alan Alexander (1992) observes a fragmentation of the system of service delivery and the demise of the 'providing' council in Scotland; Ennals and O'Brien (1990) record substantial changes as having taken place in organisational structures and roles, and that the implications of the enabling role for the future of local government are far-reaching; Wilson (1993) regards the market economy strand of Thatcherism as firmly rooted, with any deviations from it likely to be marginal.

The evidence from this research contradicts such views. Certainly if one lists the government's reforms, they are impressive numerically: universal capping and performance indicators in municipal finance; council house sales, and pick-a-landlord scheme in housing; self-governing schools and parental choice in education; a mixed economy of social care; and competitive tendering in a range of services. Evaluation of the policy impact of such initiatives requires a more qualified assessment than political rhetoric and some academic comment has offered so far.

First, let us take the financial reforms. Certainly government reforms have delivered cuts in capital spending, although recently it has been trying to protect these in public expenditure decision-making. Despite rate-capping, penalties and the poll tax, revenue spending has grown in real terms, albeit marginally. In part, this reflects the *cost* of government initiatives in the fields of fiscal reform, education administration, community care – but it also clearly reflects the political choices of local government.

We have shown that the introduction of universal capping has brought some temporary respite over spending, although in part this reflects a return to creative accounting. The Scottish Secretary is seeking further cuts in local spending through the scope for efficiency savings. This fiscal squeeze is not sustainable over a number of years without service reductions. It is fashionable to look for 'productivity gains', thus maintaining outputs at lower cost. The development of performance measurement can assist this process, as Stewart and Walsh argue, this is essentially a model sprung from production management, extensively used in production processes in Western economies. This approach is of some value in services which have a definable product, such as those already subject to competitive tendering. In the short-run, however, savings are only possible when contracts are renewable, and even these are dependent on the contractor. For services such as education, police, or social work, where the professional actually constitutes the service, productivity gains are not easy to discern. Although we can teach more school-children per teacher, provide more clients per home-help, or provide fewer policemen per thousand population, these are not productivity gains, but quality reductions. In reality, savings from labour intensive professional services can only be made by lowering staff costs or conditions of service, or by reducing the number of staff. In the shortrun, that can be accommodated by freezing appointments, early retirement, and so on, but in the long run it requires job loss. The Major government of the 1990s, like its predecessor, shows (as yet) no inclination to pursue real cuts in jobs and services.

Universal capping is a crude financial control. It removes the safety-valve of funding grant cuts from local taxation when the political consequences of change are unpalatable. In the past, the centralisation of fiscal power has always provoked unexpected and undesirable political consequences, such as tax increases, high profile service closures, or short-term creative accounting. By the 1990s, 'the principle of maximizing grant and other sources of income by seeking to evade the controls of the centre and looking for accounting loopholes was simply taken for granted . . .' (Cochrane,1993, p. 37).

The centralist approach to comparison of performance through VFM techniques is likely to face similar problems. In the absence of foolproof indicators, authorities will be able to justify their own positions convincingly. Considerable efforts will go in to creating a PI system which fails to meet its political objectives. Increased monitoring of performance threatens to swamp councils and consumers in a deluge of statistics, leading to excessive amounts of time being spent on their interpretation. The search for financial controls is unlikely to succeed when so many areas of uncertainty exist, such as the capacity to vary financial assumptions over interest rates, tax yield or wage settlements to come, or the socio-economic variables which influence performance. Budget technology still lacks the precision to make control a reality.

Market discipline, the second major area of reform, has also failed to have a significant impact. In part, this is because the number of functions subject to competitive tendering is limited, even after the planned extension, to no more than 10 per cent of all spending. Yet perceptions abound that the 'enabling authority' model has been created: even those who reject the narrow Ridley version of enabling still operate on the assumption that the conventional model of municipal provision is in demise, or inadequate, or both (see Clarke and Stewart, 1988; Ennals and O'Brien, 1990). Although the degree of competitive tendering remains small, this is not to say it has not had significant implications for staff working in the affected departments. But the anticipated large-scale savings and greater responsiveness expected by Thatcherites have not materialised. The benefits of CCT have been more in terms of clear service specifications and monitoring than financial pressures.

It is also clear that the extension of choice in education and social work is a minority experience. The reforms in those fields to date have not been on market principles, or even quasi-markets. In practice, DMS or community care is budgetary decentralisation within a continuing system of bureaucratic management. These reforms are very different from markets. For a start, despite the rhetoric of consumerism, the necessary price nexus is missing. There are certainly consumers of a professional service, but without the market tests of price. Despite the appearance and rhetoric of extensive reform, the reality is the continued dominance of municipal provision, with limited competition and limited consumer choice.

A related theme – that authorities need become more 'business- like' in their management – has hardly surfaced in Scotland. Some academic observers have been seduced by the concepts. For example:

The Government's aim of introducing the disciplines of the market and the methods of private enterprise to the management of public services has been successful and most local authorities now consider themselves as being managed rather than administered. Business planning and strategic management are increasingly part of the process of service design and delivery, especially in the large authorities.   (Alexander, A., 1992)

That some managers in contractual situations actually now adopt the *language* of business is clear to anyone in regular contact with local government. The studies which show that this is a substantive change which has permeated local politics have yet to be carried out. The surveys which show 'business planning' to be extensive are non-existent. It is one of those areas – like performance indicators – where officials are inclined to tell researchers euphemistically that they are seeking to develop it. The research which shows councillors to be adapting to this model and re-defining of their role has also yet to be carried out. Whereas the English paper on Internal Management reflected the 'enabling orientation' and advocated the need for key managerial skills in setting standards, specifying constraints, and monitoring performance, such concern was absent from its Scottish counterpart. The limited applicability of business planning models which assume clear objectives, targets and measures of performance to the local government context have been convincingly rebutted elsewhere, and need not concern us here.

Evidence of the survival of the traditional municipal provision model is indeed offered in the Scottish Office (1993c) review of internal management. After briefly considering the alternative forms of local political management, the traditional committee and departmental system survives unscathed, with local discretion over the details, and innovation left to local initiative. Despite the limited political critique of the committee system (Young, R. G., 1981), it is described as flexible and adaptable, and providing useful checks and balances. In short, despite the advocacy of 'business management' approaches, the conventional model survives.

This survival of municipal provision and the limits of market discipline do therefore raise important doubts about the wisdom of structural change. The community basis for reform is almost impossible to identify in any objective sense. In a recent paper challenging the appropriateness of this action, Ken Young was highly sceptical of the practical possibilities:

> If the policy choices which now loom can be guided by any useful reference to community attachment, it cannot be through establishing a mosaic of single-tier or unitary authorities small enough to be based on 'real communities' – assuming these can be discovered – as there is not the slightest chance that these would be large enough to be effective.   (Young, K., 1992, p. 19)

The cost assumptions, like the community assumptions, have already been shown to be dubious, and made even more so by the increase in the number of small authorities which emerged from the parliamentary process. A more costly, complex and less accountable system is on the cards. Local government reform is being proposed on the basis of questionable assumptions – on an inadequate model of local government, and to no obvious benefit, apart from Conservative political gains in political control.

The politics of opposition

The relationship between central and local government is an ongoing process of bargaining, consultation and decision- making, formalised around the government's annual cycle of legislation and resource allocation. In Scotland, this has conventionally operated on a basis of consultation and consensus building (Midwinter *et al.*, 1991, p. 91). The arrival of Thatcherism never seriously threatened to break down that relationship, despite the increased influence of ideology in the policy process, and the rhetoric of abandoning consensus. COSLA indeed shied away from breaking off relations with the Scottish Office in the Thatcher years, and has continued to participate in the formal machinery of intergovernmental relations.

The Scottish Office tradition has the additional dimension of being a territorial lobbyist, with a wider concern than simply the functions for which it is responsible, but, that apart, the territorial approach is consistent with the dominant British style of bureaucratic accommodation through consensus and avoidance of radical policy change, a style which has a functional logic:

> Consultation contributes to system maintenance not only because it imparts a sense of involvement but also because it should produce more acceptable policies. Only the wearer knows where the shoe pinches, and arguably, in giving access to interested groups and individuals the system is more effective in supplying public needs than a *dirigiste* system. Thus problem definition might be improved as a result of the wider participation by those most directly affected even if the effort and time needed to reach a decision are increased. With decisions that are specific, technical, complex, managerial, the awareness of particular circumstances is all-important. (Richardson and Jordan, 1982, p. 86)

On occasion, governments have introduced policy changes abruptly, in the pursuit of political objectives, without extensive consultation. Council house sales, the community charge, and competitive tendering are good examples. These policies were met by hostility in local government, and resistance if not non-compliance. Jordan and Richardson argue, however, that for the most part, the Thatcher government pursued policies driven by consensus rather than partisanship, the rhetoric notwithstanding. For most of the Thatcher years, there is considerable truth in this observation. The exception is the period 1987–90, when, missing the moderating influence of Willie Whitelaw, and reinforced by greater numbers of fellow travellers in positions of influence – particularly Nicholas Ridley at Environment and Michael Forsyth as a key Scottish Office minister – the government went further down the New Right agenda, with emphasis on the poll tax and competitive tendering. In the absence of extensive consultation, these reforms – challenging as they did the dominant political consensus in local government – were bound to lead to conflict.

In the Scottish policy network, however, the education, housing and social work reforms often went with the grain of professionalism rather than against. The market rhetoric notwithstanding, these reforms were managerialist rather than Thatcherite in their final forms. Extensive consultation over the devolved management of schools led to an acceptable set of reforms consistent with developments already proceeding *within* local government. These included significant differences from the English model, in that the budget was devolved to the *head teacher*, not the school board; the budget was based on actual cost, not pupil numbers and average costs; the degree of exempt categories of expenditure was enhanced; and local authorities' strategic role in determining staffing standards which had to be complied with was introduced. If there was an intention that this would facilitate 'opting out', then the results have been frustrated by public disinterest. Consultation worked:

> Having carefully considered the responses made and the very helpful and constructive suggestions put, we have clarified and revised the guidelines in a number of important respects. In particular, we have recognised the concerns of many about the very tight timescale under which implementation is to proceed. We have also extended the number of categories which need not require to be devolved to school level to include, for example, home-to-school transport, school meals and milk, and importantly, provision for special educational needs. (Ian Lang, *Hansard*, 31 March 1993, p. 318)

Considerable consensus also emerged in favour of the principles of community care, particularly with the adoption of the Griffiths Report recommendation of a lead role for social work. Indeed, though it paid the necessary homage to a mixed economy of care, it clearly favoured planning over markets in proposing to shift responsibility for DSS and the benefits system, which provided 'perverse incentives' leading to allocation by demand, not need. The result was the unplanned rapid growth of residential and nursing home care (Ministerial Statement by Malcolm Rifkind, House of Commons, 12 July 1989).

In housing, there was broad professional support for the 'planning' model advocated for housing capital investment by the Scottish Office Environment Department. This reflected experience of the existing system, and the objective of improvement in meeting housing needs, with local authorities in the key strategic and enabling role. As the Institute of Housing responded, this required the housing service: 'to retain its integrity as a primarily local authority function and the need for the strategic role to the household by staff with the necessary professional skills and expertise' (Institute of Housing in Scotland, 1993, p. 3). A related attempt to promote 'option appraisal' – a technique of investment appraisal based on cost benefit analysis used to inform capital decisions in the health service – was quickly relegated in importance in a departmental circular which stressed this as merely a first attempt to apply some of the basic principles of option appraisal to housing investment decisions, but 'the guidance is for local authorities to make use of or adopt as they see fit. Its not compulsory, and its issue does not imply a return to project control over greater intervention by the Department in monitoring local authority decisions' (ibid., p. 1).

Again, consultation worked to clarify and improve policy development. When a control agenda is imposed for partisan reasons, the potential for policy failure increases, because of the sheer impossibility of defining a policy with the necessary precision to avoid misinterpretation, or permit effective monitoring of implementation (Hood, 1976). We shall return to this later, but would like to draw attention now to the contrast between the community charge and the council tax. The former was, as I have written elsewhere:

a classic example of a bad policy, badly designed and bedevilled by problems of implementation. There was simply no recognition of the organisational, administrative and political limitations of financial

reform. In our view, the normal style of bureaucratic accommodation would not have led either to the extension of Treasury controls
or radical tax changes. Issues of feasibility and practicability would
have been raised and understood in the consultative process.
(Midwinter and Monaghan, 1993, p. 126)

The community charge reform was determined privately within
government, and consultation was confined to implementation. The
response showed overwhelming professional scepticism as to its
workability, and a preference for the stable yield, low cost and efficient
collection associated with rating. Despite political dislike of a property
tax, this remains the most feasible and relevant form of local taxation.
When the Conservatives reviewed the community charge after the fall
of Margaret Thatcher, the advice of economic theoreticians was
dispensed with, and a modified form of property tax returned,
incorporating some reforms – such as the single-person discount –
first highlighted in the Layfield Report of 1976. As we have seen, the
tax system has been defused as a political problem. The old adage that
the best tax is an old tax has been shown to have considerable
resonance.

A similar approach, regrettably, was adopted over the announcement of a commitment to a single-tier system of local government, with
consultation confined to the options, when a substantial proportion of
the public prefer the status quo. However, in this case the commitment
to a more consultative style has brought substantive changes from the
original agenda of the New Right (Adam Smith Institute, 1989;
Scottish Conservative Unionist Association, 1992), which advocated
extensive privatisation, competitive tendering, loss of functions from
local government, and a plethora of small-scale authorities. There
remain problems with the White Paper proposals, but they are more
practical than those of the Adam Smith Institute, and there will be only
a limited extension of competitive tendering, no privatisation of water,
and only a minor loss of functions from local government. That said,
the plethora of small councils is clearly at odds with professional advice
from within central and local government (Boyne *et al.*, 1994).

When consultation within the policy networks takes place on a
serious basis, then practical reforms on a consensus basis are likely. For
the most part, local government has preferred to remain in the game,
using its proposals for 'detailed negotiations with central government'
(Travers, 1993). In the late summer of 1993 COSLA announced it was

not co-operating with central government over the reform process. This in effect was sacrificing political influence, and its position was widely criticised in the media. Local authority professionals will be crucial in the changeover process, particularly if public provision is to remain effective, and employees' rights are to be protected. Sooner or later, normal service was bound to be resumed, and in effect this occurred when COSLA agreed to participate in the Staff Commission which will deal with detailed issues in the transfer of responsibility.

Opposition to the government's political agenda of fiscal control has re-emerged in the 1990s. In 1992–3, tight capping constraints were met by a combination of *creative accounting* and real savings. 'Creative accounting' is a legitimate means of bringing in financial changes which appear as 'savings' but have little real organisational impact (Parkinson, 1986). These include:

- *capitalisation* of revenue spending on maintenance into capital budget;
- *varying financial assumptions* regarding tax yield, staff turnover, grant income, and so on, as this can help avoid capping;
- *capital from current revenue* which several authorities enhanced in 1992–93 as it was excluded from the capping framework;
- *re-classification* of expenditure to the housing/water accounts from the general account to avoid capping.

Savings have been made in recent years by not filling vacancies, and cutting other discretionary budget items. A second strategy has been to *maintain organisational control*, mainly in response to CCT. Advice and experience was passed between authorities:

A Scottish Trades Unions and Local Authorities Joint Committee on Compulsory Competitive Tendering was set up with the support of COSLA and the STUC. This committee helped to formulate ground rules by which Scottish local authorities and the trades unions could co-operate to minimise the loss of employment and direct services, arising from commercial tendering. Issues such as how to avoid unwelcome cross- authority bidding, how best to provide informa- tion and training for affected workforces, and how to obtain reliable information on private contractors' methods and rates were dis- cussed in detail. In this way, a consensus emerged on how to handle potentially divisive aspects of the transition to contracted services, which has informed the process between the passage of the 1988 Act and the present. The Joint Committee was the very embodiment of a co-operative and largely effective defensive strategy to mitigate the effects of the 1988 Act, as far as this was possible under its terms. The letter of the law may have been respected, but there was no enthusiasm whatever for its provisions amongst the representative bodies of Scottish local government.   (Kerley and Wynn, 1990, p. 9)

Other authorities used the organisational changes proactively to develop work for their staff, in such ways as manufacturing windows for sale, or setting up as MOT examiners for taxis. Where it was necessary to resort to alternatives, the voluntary sector was regularly preferred to the private sector, with local authority staff involved in management structures, where possible.

In short, local government defended its turf, by concentrating on areas of uncertainty. The Labour Party advised its members to treat CCT as 'an opportunity to build up rather than undermine co-operation between councils and unions, managers and employees, and local authorities and the Conservatives'. In recent years, the proportion of staff employed on a contract basis has increased, jobs have been lost, and conditions reduced. But in the main, contracts have been retained, and direct control over provision maintained.

The case for municipal provision

Arguments for an enabling role for government reflect the New Right's predisposition to view the public sector and local government as inefficient and unresponsive in contrast with markets. The fundamental differences in the nature of public services, with their emphasis on collective consumption rather than individual buyers, the absence of price, and the lack of private provision as competition, were ignored: Local government had to become more 'business-like'.

Such advocates slowly realised the limitations of full-scale privatisation as a strategy from municipal provision. In the USA, Osborne and Gaebler (1993) have argued that the 'entrepreneurial spirit' is transforming the public sector. Much earlier, Drucker (1968) had argued for governments to govern and leave service provision to others. More recently, privatisation guru E. S. Savas (1987) urged governments to steer rather than to row. The American experience, however, as captured by Osborne and Gaebler, is similar to the British advocacy of contracting out, greater funding by user charges, and performance measurement. Certainly the book has an infectious enthusiasm, but it is at best investigative journalism rather than analysis. It relies on anecdotes and case studies, partially explored, with no wider body of evidence to support the case being made. No serious exposition of the weakness of public provision, the benefits of contracting out, or the capacity of performance measurement is provided. Caveats are occasionally made, and these often undermine the whole basis of their argument. For example, they log the problems of contracting-out, including 'low-ball bids' the danger of private monopolies, and simple fraud and then conclude that contracting out works best 'when public agencies can define precisely what they want done, generate competition for the job, evaluate a contractor's performance, and replace or penalize those who fail to achieve expected performance levels' (Osborne and Gaebler, 1993, p. 89).

As we have seen, these conditions are relevant only to a small proportion of local authority activities – mainly the manual services with a measurable product. They are of little relevance to mainstream professional services such as education, police, or social work. In Scotland, the impact of the 1988 competitive tendering legislation on local authority staffing has been to increase the proportion of staff on a contract basis from 8 per cent in 1989–90 to 20.6 per cent in 1993–94. Local authority staffing levels, however, remained broadly stable in the 1990s, with the large drop in 1993–94 reflecting the transfer of college staff from local to central government (Table 6.1).

Table 6.1 *Budgeted manpower in Scottish local authorities*

Fiscal year	Budgeted manpower
1990–91	193 611
1991–92	196 173
1992–93	195 955
1993–94	188 467

Source: *Rating Review* (various).

With the mainstream professional services (education, social work, police and fire) accounting for over 50 per cent of manpower totals, the limitations for extending CCT are clear enough.

Similar problems arise when consideration of the scope for charging for services directly is also considered. Osborne and Gaebler (1993) argue that:

> User fees are not always appropriate, of course. They work under three conditions; when the service is primarily a 'private good' benefiting the individuals who use it; when those who don't pay for it can be excluded from enjoying its benefits; and when fees can be collected efficiently. 'Collective goods' which benefit society at large should not be charged in full to paying customers.   (p. 204)

In practice, few public services are pure private goods, and certainly the strict division into the classificatory scheme of economists would be difficult. Therefore these matters are resolved by simple political judgement, not the canons of economic efficiency. The scope and extent of public services is a central political question which entails social as well as economic values. Thus though we could levy a price for refuse collection on each household or business, there are intangible public benefits from the effective collection and disposal of refuse, which are not amenable, without heroic assumptions, to the economist's calculus. The extensive application of charges would have fundamental redistributive consequences, as some 20 per cent of council tax income is in the form of DSS rebates.

There has been considerably less progress in expanding charges for services than in expanding competitive tendering (see Table 6.2). These years were the high watermark of municipal Thatcherism, yet charges remained broadly stable. As with other theoretically driven policies, their scope for practical application has not proven great, rather they are used as a useful short-term device in periods of fiscal constraint.

Table 6.2   *Income from fees and charges*

	£m.	% LA income
1987–88	223	5.0
1988–89	288	5.9
1989–90	277	5.3
1990–91	280	5.2

Source: Scottish Local Government Finance Statistics,
Scottish Office.

As Osborne and Gaebler note: 'User fees have two advantages: they raise money, and they lower demand for public services: Both help balance public budgets' (p. 204). Not all aspects of municipal services are amenable to charging. One such area, public libraries, experienced a growth in fee income from 2.6 per cent of the total to 5.7 per cent between 1980 and 1987. However, contrary to economic theory, these charges were raised to promote service development, not curtail demand (Midwinter and McVicar, 1992, p. 74).

Finally, we would argue that to conduct arguments about charging in terms of economic efficiency – as do the New Right – is to ignore the problems of practical politics. In practice, the measurement of 'external benefits' is fraught with difficulties (Bailey, 1988) and is peripheral to the concerns of political decision-making. Concepts developed at a high level of abstraction can neither explain nor 'improve' decisions. Charges are often held up as a means of curtailing the very demand that 'free' public provision seeks to promote. It seems to us that the theoretical arguments about the absence of price in municipal provision are at best, not proven and at worst, irrelevant to the real world of political choice.

So far, we have examined the negative case for municipal provision – that the policy instruments for making it more market-orientated are of limited practical application. To make the positive case, we must turn to the field of evaluation, using recent attitude surveys.

One study in the USA (Goodsell, 1990) argues forcibly that, in stark contrast with right-wing theory or popular press horror stories, citizens have a far more favourable perception of public services than their critics recognise:

> Direct reports from citizens on their experiences with bureaucracy – as distinct from generalized conventional wisdom on the subject – indicate that they perceive far more good than bad in their daily interactions with it. Client polls, public opinion surveys, exit interviews, and mailed questionnaires all repeat the basic finding that the majority of encounters are perceived as satisfactory. Bureaucracy is reported as usually providing the services sought and expected. Most of the time it lives up to acceptable standards of efficiency, courtesy and fairness. (p. 139)

One major study of citizen attitudes was carried out for the British government in 1986. It concluded 'levels of satisfaction with local government remain high', with more than 70 per cent of the sample being satisfied with the performance of the local authorities (Young, K., 1986, pp. 99–100). This study has been updated and extended by Bloch and John (1991), and this provides highly relevant data for our concerns, as it assesses attitudes to the reforms we have examined. This found a high level of satisfaction (82 per cent) with the way respondents' local council ran things. This research revealed only limited support for contracting out, and that the level of support in Scotland for municipal provision was higher than elsewhere at 79 and 81 per cent for parks and cleansing services respectively, while 70 per cent favoured the continuing local provision of housing. Bloch and John concluded: 'Most people would rather local government was responsible for the running and providing of local services than other public or private organisations. These findings indicate little support for the policy of contracting-out introduced by the 1988 Local Government Act' (p. 77).

This demonstrates the real gap that exists between the political agenda of the right and the public it serves. We noted in our discussion of education reforms that the public does not necessarily share either the bureaucratic power or the bureaucratic inefficiency interpretations of professionalism that are central to New Right thinking. It is this hard-headed realism that provides the best evidence that Thatcherism has had much less impact in practice than its rhetoric suggests. The local welfare state – as much as the welfare state (Cochrane, 1993) – has survived the political onslaught. Support for municipal Thatcherism remains tepid in Scotland in contrast with more managerialist reforms. Support for the council tax is now over 50 per cent, far greater than ever achieved by the Thatcherite poll tax; opposition to water privatisation was even higher, at over 90 per cent; only 31 per cent of Scots favoured the provision for self-governing schools; and only 29 per cent favoured the 'pick-a-landlord' scheme. In short, support for municipal provision remains strong, despite a decade of legislation to reduce its scope and power, and the high political profile given to arguments regarding its efficiency. People have positive views about their municipal services in general. This is not to deny the very real problems some people face in dealing with local authorities – which may well be problems of policy and practice rather than the result of the system – but simply to note that despite the very real human problems which find their way into the local press – which induce comments on bureaucracy run amok – for the majority of us, local authorities provide a comprehensive range of services to our general satisfaction, and the critique of the right has had little impact on those views simply because of its theoretical basis and limited practical relevance. Criticism of municipal provision is not of course the preserve of the right. John Stewart has a record of sustained criticism of the fragmentation and service orientation of traditional local government. From a policy analysis perspective, he regards the manifestation of traditional organisation – functionalism, hierarchy and uniformity – as inadequate for local government, resulting in unresponsiveness to changing needs, incrementalism, lack of strategy and policy review, departmentalism (Stewart, J., 1971) and the need for a corporate approach and authority wide culture.

Stewart's consistent desire is to reduce the emphasis on service delivery and enhance the governmental dimension. Like all advocates of change, he overstates – perhaps deliberately – the strength of his case and the weakness of professionalism. Stewart has always had a 'greater vision' of local government than the classical model. As Cochrane observed:

> Until the mid 1970s, local government appeared to be a relatively unproblematic part of the British political system, despite attempts to 'modernize' it in the late 1960s and early 1970s. Its task was to deliver a fairly clearly defined set of services at local level, reasonably efficiently, and with a degree of democratic accountability.
> (Cochrane, 1993, p. 8)

Stewart's critique, however, is 'the launch pad' for a political theory of local government, based on an active citizenry, in which decentralisation of service delivery is combined with a governing role for the authority. John Stewart's authority is an 'assertive authority' concerned with the 'overall economic, cultural and physical well-being of the local community' in which strategic planning provides a basis for better decision-making. Representative democracy should be supplemented and improved through proportional representation, referendum, citizens' meetings and an elected political executive (Clarke and Stewart, 1991).

Similar arguments about professionalism and the committee system have been made in a Scottish context by Ronald Young, although he is dismissive of the need for strategic planning and policy analysis. For Young, there is a need for greater political and public involvement in decision-making and he sees 'over-professionalisation' as the 'central problem' of local government (1993). Expertise gives professionals influence and control, although Young is equally sceptical of the 1980s breed of corporate managers whose activities consist largely of 'taking in the professionals' washing'. Political change is difficult to achieve because of 'certain deep-rooted traditions and values e.g. organisational hierarchies; belief in the uniformity of services; and respect for professional 'expertise'; all of these and more are advanced by the committee system' (ibid., p. 57).

For Young, the key role of the politician in local government is to shake the authority out of its lethargy and give it a sense of direction. Although in theory, political leadership is the norm, in practice, councillors are 'mere rubber stamps' and policies are driven by government or professional advice. Only in the post-reorganisation period have

> left-wing councillors devoted more attention to the formulation of manifestos, have attempted to assert local party strength as at least a countervailing force against a bureaucratic and professional system which so insidiously co-opts councillors . . . (Young, R. G., 1981, p. 17)

He sees an ever increasing professionalisation of policy-making, reflected in a surfeit of policy-planning documents such as regional reports, structure plans, housing plans and transport policies and programmes, which

- are increasingly compartmentalised;
- have a technical bias;
- are professional in origin; and
- are increasingly arid.

The end result is 'a volume of jargon which is so daunting that very few politicians ever bother to read the documents' (p. 17).

The failure of comprehensive planning in government has been well recorded elsewhere. The importance of such plans is not their scientificity but that they are bids for resources which provide an interface for negotiation with the centre. At a technical level, they *must* demonstrate competence and sophistication, but this is not to deny the importance – in the final analysis – of political judgement. These are aids to decision-making, not techniques.

Young however, sees professionalism as an obstacle to innovation, sustained by the organisational system. 'The committee process itself, with its predetermined agendas, its rules of procedure, its focus upon itemised decision-making at the expense of policy-making too often becomes a chivalrous ritual, a substitute for real action' (ibid., p. 18). He makes the following criticisms that committees:

• are too big for creative exploration of ideas;
• are too concerned with taking decisions;
• encourage collusion between chairman and chief officers;
• are too prone to inertia;
• are under professional control; and
• are too concerned with professional issues.

Young's critique is reflective of his impatience with the culture of service delivery in local government and his own interest in community development. In short, Young sees local government not as a vehicle for local service delivery, but as a mechanism of social change, encouraging community development and challenges to bureaucracy. When he goes on to discuss the development of member-officer working groups and area management in Strathclyde, his observations simply 'assume' these lead to better decisions than the committee system approach. Although he sees this as an 'exciting dynamic', he offers only one example of policy change which 'produced questions and recommendations which otherwise would not have materialised' (p. 20), although he does not explain why professionalism would not have generated such a response if left to its own devices. One suspects his own admission that 'reformers always have to simplify and exaggerate' is true in his own case, as he fails to present the evidence necessary to reach judgements about the _causal_ connection between the process of decision-making and outcomes.

This indeed is the problem with most reformist tracts, whether advocating strategic management, political control, or public participation in decision-making. They 'assume' change will result in a better 'quality' of decision, which cannot be measured – the same failing as the right's assumptions about competition and choice. Only by analysing needs and service provision can particular decisions be evaluated. Evaluating the process is like watching a football match without goalposts.

Hambleton and Hogget (1990) also advocate decentralisation and consumerism as part of the agenda of the 'radical democratic left'. Left and right argue that the state has

> become overly bureaucratic, remote from the needs of many of the people it is meant to address and that it has become the servant of powerfully entrenched producer interests rather than the users of these services.   (p. 104)

The bureaucratic paternalism thesis suffers the same problems as the New Right thesis. What is meant by 'producer interests'? The answer of the left to the 'problem' is 'public involvement' and 'improvement'. They argue that there is a need to strengthen the voice of the citizen, not merely through consultation but to 'participate in management'. They see participatory democracy as

> rooted in the organisations of civil society, organisations which are essentially associated in form. There is an immense variety of such organisations, some with a handful of members, others, like the National Trust, with millions. They include everything from groups formed by women or people with disabilities to environmental and heritage groups   (p. 110)

Thus the 'renewal' of political democracy involves both improving and extending existing representative systems and developing participatory democracy. The rhetoric – for such it is – is that this will 'strengthen' democratic control. It may, but that is not self-evident, and whilst consultation may bring benefits of responsiveness, it has little to offer for strategic choice and determining priorities. Hambleton and Hogget's list of options for strengthening voice include some developments already taking place, but others look hopelessly utopian (for example, voter registration drives). At heart, this is a plea for an active citizenry – or at least a wish that people were more like themselves. In practice, school boards, community councils, and tenants associations all have difficulty in attracting active members. They are also not necessarily representative and are not necessarily any more democratic than elected councillors. More importantly, like the New Right's agenda, this is one which operates at the margins of municipal activities. There is a sense of *déjà vu* – in the attempts to recreate the corporate planning/decentralisation agenda of the 1970s in the business planning/participation agenda of the 1990s – with a dash of consumerism thrown in. Thus the main difficulty

> lies in ensuring the whole of the public is involved – the naturally articulate and influential sections of a community are unlikely to be representative of everyone. If you simply set up a committee of local people, you are unlikely to take full account of the needs of the less vocal, who tend to be those most in need of council support. Worse, if you empower the articulate people, they will often disempower the others. Empowerment is an attractive concept but great care is needed to put it into practice. (Bonner and McConnell, 1993, p. 119)

Part of the professional critique lies in the traditional dislike of departmentalism and part in the discovery of consumerism. Such reforms do not have an impressive record, and often represent form rather than substance. The danger is, as with market systems, they are set up and people assume the system is 'more efficient' as a result. If they generate complaints which cannot be satisfied because of policy or resource constraints, they will become sources of grievances from the activist minority. As with the New Right's critique, the diagnosis and solution are both wanting.

However, the 1990s have brought a refreshing reappraisal of the performance of professionalism. As Rhodes (1992) observes, Stewart's critique of professionalism offers no account of the strengths of professionalism, including expertise, continuity and reliability. Professionalism in local government did not grow from any grand theory of local government. Municipal provision developed in a piecemeal and pragmatic way - and the overwhelming evidence is still of a high level of general satisfaction with performance. Professionalism has managed the rapid expansion of the local welfare state from 1945 to 1975 and has helped manage the crisis and constraints since then (Travers, 1993). Both right and left have an activist view of local citizens, whereas in reality

> it is questionable whether most users want to be empowered to the extent of participating in the running of services. When users were asked whether the organisations responded to their needs for consultation and empowerment, most had difficulty in even conceptualising the question. They were, for the most part, happy to

have the running of public services to those trained and paid to do so.   (Beale and Pollitt, 1994, p. 17)

A robust defence of the classical model was made recently in a report by the Local Government Management Board (LGMB) in England (1994). In *Fitness for Purpose*, they examine strategic choices over roles which local authorities face, and identify four broad patterns. These are:

- the service provision approach (or classical model);
- the commercial approach;
- the community governance approach;
- the neighbourhood approach.

These fall broadly into the enabling model, and the participation models discussed earlier: the commercial approach is seen to combine a view of the value of market mechanisms with an individualistic perspective and a service-dominated conception of local governance; the community governance approach stresses a comprehensive governmental role using market mechanisms as appropriate; the neighbourhood approach places a strong emphasis on community at the more local level of the neighbourhood in small towns. It may be that such approaches are commonplace south of the border but in Scotland, this is simply an additional dimension which supports the service provision model, which regards the role of the market as limited, and the essential political choices remain over the extent and pattern of services and the level of resources. As the LGMB noted:

> There is great strength in the traditional approach to local governance and service delivery. This approach can and should be revised to pay greater attention to the needs of customers. There is scope for the introduction of market mechanisms, but the scope should not be overemphasized. The introduction of such mechanisms should not be used as a reason for the radical redesign of organisational structures, processes and personnel policies, which should remain rooted in an ethos of direct public provision.   (LGMB, 1994, para. 2.17)

This questioning of the realism of client-contractor splits, in the case of external contractors, remains dominant in Scotland. Local authority structures remain essentially those of service department/committee links with integrating resource departments and committees. There is scepticism of the need for change over tried and tested methods, and any change will in the main be gradual, not radical. As with England:

> Single-service based departments seek to harness the benefits of professional knowledge and experience, which may be diluted by merging departments or replacing specialist units with generic teams. Corporate strategies may tend to emphasize resource allocation among services, rather than council-wide objectives that transcend familiar service categories. Clear management hierarchies should ensure that everyone knows who does what and where responsibility lies.   (para. 31.8)

The parallels between the old convention of corporate planning and the new business planning are clear enough – professionalism remains important, and service delivery remains a high political concern. In a sense, these authorities do not need to get 'back to basics'. They have been protecting basics all along, supporting traditional values of public provision within a democratic framework.

It is time, then, for reconsideration of those critiques of local government. Both are at best peripheral to the main problems of service delivery in a framework of political accountability. The enabling model, the governing model, or the participatory model, are better seen as complementary mechanisms to the classical model, than as alternatives to it. Despite the welter of rhetoric, the image of radical reform, the language of the new public management, the glitz of marketing and public relations, the central role of the local authority remains – municipal provision of services.

> For most authorities, the service range is little different from the 1970s. Councils are still major providers of housing, personal social services, schools and conventional services. The numbers employed by local authorities have not altered significantly during a period when central government engaged in a relentless onslaught against revenue and capital expenditure. Town and country halls are still the centre of local political life.   (Travers, 1993, p. 1).

What implications does this have for the Conservative agenda of reform? Faulty diagnosis can result in poor, or irrelevant solutions. What needs to be done?

The case for the Wheatley system

The Conservative approach to the reform of local government is concerned with issues of process and structure. By redefining the role of the local authority as an enabling one concerned with strategic choice and monitoring performance, the government believes it has weakened the case for the large regional authorities and opened the door to a system of smaller authorities more directly related to concepts of community.

In practice, the concept of community provides little useful guidance to a sensible basis for redrawing the geography of local government. That people have a weak attachment to the administrative areas of local government is not a new phenomenon. It existed in the pre-1975 system also. Recent evidence in a Department of the Environment survey confirms this, finding that people

> usually knew the name of their local authority, but we found that the boundaries of local authority areas did not typically seem very familiar or important, unless they happen to coincide with some emotionally more significant area. It was not the local government element that people seemed to identify with, but the underlying sense of clan or community with which a specific geographical area might be imbued.   (quoted in K. Young, 1992)

The government has stressed the need to balance the issue of community identity with the need for efficiency, but it has interpreted efficiency in narrow, administrative terms and assumed that operational efficiency will be unaffected – except in the case of police and fire services, where the status quo is maintained in the interests of efficiency; and in water and sewerage, where three new public authorities are created in the interests of efficiency. Inconsistency is the order of the day. Fortunately, the limited relevance of community attachments to the organisation of municipal authorities has been accepted.

The Wheatley Report proposals had a degree of administrative logic. The report was concerned with functional efficiency, and argued for large-scale authorities based on a city and its hinterland in urban areas, and broader geographic areas in rural Scotland, with responsibility for the major municipal services. Amenity and environmental services offered little operational advantages if organised on a large scale, and hence these were allocated to the districts. Wheatley's logic was weakened by the parliamentary process, particularly by allocating housing to district authorities, but nevertheless a rationale for structure existed. Reflecting the prevailing planning mood, Wheatley advocated a two-tier system with a new regional level of government which linked urban and rural Scotland, and facilitated integrated planning, covering land- use, transportation, housing and infrastructure. In addition, an economies-of-scale argument was advanced for regional authorities which would permit more efficient use of resources and the provision of a comprehensive range of specialist services. Arguments for regional-ism, then, recognise that area-wide problems of government require an administrative unit to match. Strategic planning and functional efficiency would be achieved through regions.

It is difficult to see any rationale in the new structure. Several small authorities with populations of less than 100 000 are created, whilst the remainder are considerably larger. Downs and Larkey (1986) argue that reorganisations are frequently promoted as efficiency reforms, when in reality they seek to promote political advantage. Just such a rationale for the present reforms was made to the author in private correspondence by a retired senior civil servant from the Scottish Office who was concerned at the Conservative agenda. He wrote:

> The background to the current administration's interest in local government reform, as is pretty widely known, is party political and little more. It irks some government supporters to see such a microscopic number of Scottish local authorities in Tory hands, and from time to time they agitate for restructuring which they see as giving the prospect of a few more.

McVicar *et al.* (1994), after exhaustive research, show that dislike of the Labour power fiefdoms was a prime source of Conservative Party discontent with the present structure. Despite the alleged loyalty to old counties, these are regularly subdivided to reflect the Conservative's political interests. This political rationale is the only way to make sense of the creation of small authorities in the light of the continuing reality of municipal provision remaining the dominant mode of service delivery in the new system.

The end result is a system of fewer authorities. Unlike previous reorganisations, consolidation is *not* into large authorities, but into smaller units for the administration of the key regional services. Ostensibly, reform ushers in a unitary structure, but the major structural change is the dismantling of the large regional authorities, although recognising that a regional level continues to exist through a plethora of appointed water and sewerage boards, joint police and fire boards, or joint committees – a return to 'the administrative duplication and confusion of the 19th Century' (Brooke, 1984, pp. 84–5).

Indeed, no better statement of the case for regional authorities has been made than the plethora of observations in the White Paper on the need for joint arrangements between the new smaller authorities. These include the following:

Education
Already some councils make arrangements with others for the provision of some of the more specialist services – this is likely to continue.   (para. 3.8)

Social Work
The government expects that the smaller new authorities may also choose to purchase certain specialist services from larger authorities. (para. 3.9)

Children's Reporter Service
The Reporter is a chief officer of the local authority and responsible for a department containing reporters and support staff. If these arrangements were retained under the new local authority structure, there would be a significant number of authorities which would only be able to justify departments of about two reporters. This would have major implications for the efficiency, consistency of professional practice and the costs of the Reporter service. The government therefore consider that the Reporter service will be more effectively provided as a national service and it is proposed to set up a new body responsible for providing the Reporter service to children's hearings throughout Scotland.   (para. 3.11)

Police and Fire
The current number of police forces and fire brigades will be retained. It is, however, proposed that provision be made in the Bill to align existing police and fire areas with the boundaries of the new councils and to establish joint committees where police forces and fire brigades cover more than one council area.   (para. 3.12)

Emergency Planning and Civil Defence
In some areas, however, a greater degree of co-ordinated planning
for emergencies will be required, and the new authorities will have to
link their planning activities with those of the emergency services and
of neighbouring local authorities.   (para. 3.13)

Roads
The continuation of structure planning means that a general
framework will also be available to allow authorities to co-ordinate
local road and transport schemes across council boundaries where
necessary.   (para. 3.15)

Planning
The Secretary of State intends to take powers in the Bill to specify
those areas where he considers that a structure plan should cover
more than one local authority. He will expect the authorities in those
areas to work together to prepare and maintain such structure
plans.   (para. 3.19)

Water and Sewerage
the best structure for these services in Scotland will be achieved by
establishing three public water authorities.   (para. 3.22)

Cultural Activities and Library Services
local authorities will also need to give careful consideration to the
continuation and extension of the various forms of voluntary joint
arrangements.   (para. 3.28)

Relations with the European Union
there will be a need, particularly when local authorities are seeking to
provide input into the development of European policy, for them to
group together to equip themselves with as strong a voice as
possible.   (para. 3.37)

Trading Standards and Environmental Health
As in other area, where it would not be economic for every authority
to employ its own specialists, the government believe that the new
councils will be able to establish effective co-operation and
purchasing arrangements where these are required.   (para. 3.35)

Valuation

The Secretary of State is proposing that there should be no increase in the number of assessors as a result of reorganisation. He intends therefore to take power to specify those areas covered by more than one new authority for which he considers a single assessor should be appointed.   (para. 3.37)

The notion that the new system will be a unitary one is a myth. It will not be simpler, with clearer accountability and better co-ordination. On close examination, what is being proposed is a *fragmentation* of service responsibility through the use of appointed boards, joint boards, joint arrangements and inter-authority contracting. These are weaker models of service delivery than the direct provision achieved in the present system.

The erosion of local democracy

Abstract theories of accountability, whether of the market or participatory variant, do not provide a sound basis for political decisions about local government. Representative democracy in Britain did not develop in response to grand theory, but as a pragmatic means of citizen influence. The attraction of the local authority model as a mechanism of accountability is that it permits direct responsibility within a framework of local choice (Regan and Stewart, 1982). The enabling authority model seeks to enhance market accountability, as did the poll tax. The problem with the White Paper proposals is the *fragmentation* of accountability:

> The growing complexity of government has made it more difficult to identify who is accountable for what. The fragmentation of urban government symbolised by the division of the county borough's powers in the 1974 reorganisation between county, district, health and water authorities, has made the fields of accountability for closely inter-related activities difficult to identify.   (Stewart, J. D., 1982, p. 21)

In the Scottish context, these observations are of considerable relevance, as there is now a more fragmented network of governmental agencies, joint boards, and contractual arrangements in addition to local authorities and health boards.

There are two levels of government in Britain, and two models of accountability. Political accountability at the centre operates through parliamentary accountability. The government and its ministers are accountable for their stewardship of their departments to parliament, and to the wider public through the electoral and the representative process. Sometimes service delivery is carried out directly by civil service departments, sometimes through agencies staffed by professionals and supervised by members appointed by ministers and accountable to them. Increasingly, this accountability is formalised through a managerialist model involving business plan, annual report and accounts, and policy review. The local authority model is the alternative, operating at a local level with a governing body of laymen, elected by the public at large, to control a system managed by professionals (Regan and Stewart, 1982). The main difference is that departments and bodies operate services within a policy and resource framework determined by the government, wherea local government has a degree of policy autonomy and fiscal powers.

The reforms have the effect of reducing this range of powers and weakening the links of accountability in local government. For aspects of some services, such as roads, social services, further education and water and sewerage in Scotland, *political* accountability is transferred to ministers, operating either through their departments of appointed boards. For other services, political accountability is weakened by the need for joint arrangements for police, fire and aspects of planning and transport. Joint boards are widely acknowledged to be problematic. Decisions concerning the area of a component authority can be taken by a majority located elsewhere. This results in a fragmentation of responsibility in which clear lines of accountability are lost. Decision-makers are not directly accountable to local voters. In short, the structural changes, with their reliance on joint arrangements, fall far short of the clear accountability offered under direct municipal provision in the present system. Accountability, however, is not delivered by structure alone – it must be considered in the wider context.

The Conservative interpretation of accountability has been mainly an economic one, linked to paying for services. The creation of small authorities in part reflects disaffection for redistributive spending pursued by regional authorities. It is a reflection of their limited view of government, and it does not fit easily with mainstream public opinion in Scotland. The problem with the enabling model is its limited application: municipal provision is not simply about efficient delivery, it is about delivery in response to *need*, not the ability and willingness to pay which characterises consumers in markets. As a political institution, local government reflects community choices for providing services which we do not necessarily consume ourselves, but which we 'value' nevertheless. The participatory model neglects the fact that 'the majority of citizens have neither the time nor the inclination to be generalists in public affairs' (Rhodes, 1987b, p. 70).

The government argues that its structural reforms will promote accountability by clarifying responsibility. Such clarification is indeed a desirable element of any reform of local government, but is has been invoked in a narrow sense, meaning simply the allocation of functions to a unitary authority. The government claim to be promoting efficiency and accountability through the enabling authority concept, whereby authorities no longer provide services themselves but 'enable' others to provide them (Ridley, 1988). Local authorities have in fact always made use of the private and voluntary sectors as appropriate. However, the benefits of municipal provision by professionals have been ignored, and the capacity for extending the private sector exaggerated. In many key aspects of education, social work, police and fire, the quality and expertise required simply do not exist in the private sector. 'Professionals are a source of expertise' (Rhodes, 1992), and this specialist knowledge cannot be delivered by or left to market forces. It has required public provision to *ensure* its development.

Market accountability is not an adequate basis for local government. In a representative democracy, accountability requires 'policy accountability' for strategies adopted and the decisions taken, and it also involves the direct accountability of the individual representative of his or her community for his or her efforts on their behalf. Competitive tendering does not enhance accountability – it can frustrate and delay the potential for political intervention to deal with emerging issues, as arguments over contract specifications are ironed out.

Autonomy and accountability are twin elements of a healthy local democracy. Autonomy refers to the 'power of localities to function free from the oversight authority of higher tiers of state' (Clark, 1984, p. 195). It is the capacity for autonomous action which facilitates accountability, and makes it meaningful.

These reforms have also to be considered in terms of the Conservatives' constitutional initiative, known as 'Taking Stock'. The arrival of Ian Lang at the Scottish Office brought a more consultative style of government, with ministers acknowledging that they had been abrasive towards Scots in the Thatcher years, and that they needed a less partisan approach which pursued policies acceptable to the majority of Scots (Fraser, 1992; Lang, 1992). Some of the policy innovations in the 1990s do indeed reflect that commitment: water has not been privatised; education and social work reforms have been more managerialist than Thatcherite, representing administrative decentralisation rather than privatisation; the council tax replaced the Thatcherite poll tax and has found acceptability. Policies such as opting-out of schools, however remain controversial and unpopular in Scotland. In general, however, the approach is less partisan, with the major exception of reshaping local authorities. This was presented as part of a commitment to decentralise power.

> The Government's plans for the reform of local government are at the heart of the strategy to press decision-making downwards. The new single-tier, all-purpose authorities will be better able to promote effectively the interests of the areas they represent. They will be more accountable to the people who live there. In sum, they will reflect the diversity of Scotland as a whole and revive the dynamism of local democracy. (Scottish Office, 1993b, p. 36)

However, the problem is that the abolition of the large regional authorities would facilitate the creation of a devolved parliament with legislative *and* executive powers which 'Taking Stock' is intended to prevent. Once the new system is established, the easiest way to effect democratic control and promote functional efficiency would be to 'centralise' responsibility for police, fire, water and sewerage, roads, education and social work, rather than to engage on a further redrawing of the local government map to provide reasonably- sized authorities in the interests of efficiency. Similar proposals have already been made by the SNP and the Liberal Democrats, and Labour too is committed to a single-tier system of local government, with joint arrangements if necessary, and which also creates city-based authorities. The prospect is that parliamentary devolution of power would become executive centralisation of power, once the limitations of small authorities become clear. The future prospects for local democracy are not great. When the reform package is viewed as a whole, it is one of decline and fiscal autonomy. The promise of a simpler, more accountable system is not fulfilled.

It is clear that the central assumption of reform is flawed. Local authorities may develop their enabling role, but they will and should remain important mechanisms of service delivery. The government has failed to provide a convincing case against municipal provision. Indeed, such evidence as exists clearly shows continuing municipal provision has widespread public support.

Local government requires a structure which facilitates efficiency and democratic control irrespective of developments in Scotland's governance. The present system has been subject to unsubstantiated criticism, much in the way the rating system was in the 1980s. A badly conceived reform like the present White Paper will merely ensure that the issue of local government structure remains politically divisive. Ironically, the second Consultation Paper, *Shaping the New Authorities,* did set out an option which would have gone some way to meeting the government's stated objectives on efficiency and accountability: a structure based on fifteen units which retained all the existing regional and islands councils except Strathclyde, which would be subdivided broadly on the existing health board areas. This option would have maximised the potential for efficiency gains and minimised the need for joint arrangements; it would have arguably promoted accountability.

Although supplementary mechanisms to enhance consultation and to promote consumer choice as appropriate are welcome, the essence of representative democracy remains the exercise of broad political choice between services, areas and groups.

The Conservative agenda for local government reflected its political philosophy on the role of the state. It saw a need for lower spending and taxation, and greater use of market mechanisms to enhance efficiency. Municipal Thatcherism in practice was modified by the constraints of the political system – its application to local government was limited, and remains so. Although the Major administration retains elements of market rhetoric, it has returned to a more pragmatic approach in practice. There has not been a revolution in local government, and the government has shifted away from the mainstream agenda. The poll tax has been abandoned, little extension of charging for services has taken place, and the enabling authority model has been constrained by its limited applicability to municipal provision. The emphasis has now shifted to limited consumer choice within a bureaucratically managed approach to budgetary decentralisation, and a return to conventional Treasury centralism in terms of fiscal controls. Together these things seriously undermine the case for change in structure if municipal provision remains the predominant form of service delivery. The need for larger local authorities to provide the major services remains.

The reform of local government has been bedevilled by the competing notions of market and participatory democracy of right and left, whose alternatives are at best useful adjuncts to the existing system rather than alternatives. Cochrane's (1993) concept of local government as delivering services efficiently with a degree of local accountability is worth retaining. Local government should be reviewed and criticised for what it is, not for failing to meet the aspirations of political theorists or activists as a mechanism of social and economic change. As Goodsell (1990) wrote, 'it is the humdrum, daily routine of bureaucracy that determines its efficiency for citizens' (p. 149).

Public support for local government as an institution and satisfaction with its services remains high. Forty two per cent of citizens believe that central control has increased, but only a minority (19 per cent) support that change. Scots tended to dislike central government fiscal controls, and were unconvinced by the arguments for competitive tendering. In short, despite the often referred to decline in political consensus, a public consensus remains in favour of the welfare state and of local government as the mechanism for delivery.

The new system will be capable of delivering services effectively, albeit at a higher cost and perhaps with some loss of specialist services. It will not be a policy disaster a la poll tax. Professionals will ensure continuity despite the administrative and political problems. However, the reform proposals do not promote a sound basis for local government in the next century. If implemented, they will merely ensure that the structure has to be reconsidered by another government in the not-too-distant future and that may lead to even further centralisation to a devolved Parliament. By contrast, the Wheatley system of large regional authorities for strategic services and small district authorities for amenity services remains a sensible relevant division of powers today which retains political choice at a more local level. A reform which cannot guarantee efficiency savings, and which fragments accountability, cannot be positively welcomed. The reform does, however, look likely to go ahead, and it is sensible to begin now to address the problems ahead.

7 Problems of Implementation

Introduction

In this final chapter, we shall explore some of the issues the government will face in implementing its new system. This reform is proceeding in a hostile political climate, unlike its predecessor. At the time of writing (September, 1994) COSLA is still refusing to co-operate in the implementation of the reforms. The public remain unconvinced of the case for structural change in local government, and are over-whelmingly opposed to the removal of water from local control.

Concern with problems of implementation in modern government, with its dispersal of power between agencies and units of local government, grew in the 1980s. Faced with a mainly sceptical group of local professionals and politicians, the prospects for *successful* implementation in this case are not good. Three issues have the potential to create adverse political consequences for the government. These are:

- the removal of water from local government;
- the transfer of functions to the new authorities;
- the cost implications of reform.

We shall examine each of these in turn.

The problem of Scotland's water

The decision to restructure Scotland's local authorities created an additional problem for the government. Whereas in England water boards had been created in 1974, the same reorganisation in Scotland left water and sewerage as local authority functions. The structure in Scotland had undergone rationalisation since the war, when there were 210 water authorities in Scotland – mostly provided independently by

142

councils, but also including six boards and two non- statutory water companies. In 1967, the services were allocated to thirteen single-purpose regional water boards to facilitate planning and efficiency. All board members were local elected representatives. A similar process of rationalisation took place in sewerage, although it was never located in boards.

In England, both water and sewerage services were transferred to ten regional water authorities in 1974, and governed by a combination of councillors and central government appointees. In 1983, these became wholly appointed by the Secretary of State, with consumer interests vested in consultative committees. Privatisation followed in 1989, with ten water and sewerage companies, and twenty-nine water companies operating within a framework regulated by the Secretary of State, the National Rivers Authority, and the Office for Water Services. No indication of extending privatisation to Scotland was made by ministers at this stage. Privatisation in England was followed by large price increases, and a growth in disconnections, from 2524 in 1989 to 7662 in 1991 (Accounts Commission, 1992). In Scotland, water charges also rose in this period, in part because of shortfalls in community charge collection (Black, 1994). Nevertheless, Scottish public opinion was strongly anti-privatisation: a MORI poll in 1992 showed 7 per cent in favour, with 90 per cent opposed.

The government published a consultation paper on the future of water and sewerage services in November 1992 (Scottish Office, 1992). It argued that the reform of local government made it necessary to decide how these services should be provided in the future, and to consider new ways of financing and managing them. There was a concern to pursue business practice, observe high environmental standards, and contain costs for consumers. The report recorded the extensive range of controls on water and sewerage authorities, on water quality and the treatment of sewerage. European Community directives also constrained the authorities, in particular through the Drinking Water Directive, the Bathing Water Directive, and the Urban Waste Water Treatment Directive, through the setting of standards. In addition, authorities must meet the standards of the river purification authority for the area.

These standards created imperatives for investment to meet the demands of such controls, and a potential cost of £5billion (ibid., p. 17). The government therefore set itself three key objectives for delivery of services:

- the highest quality;
- the lowest possible cost to the consumer; while
- maintaining and improving safeguards for the environment.

These would require both a major capital investment programme and the promoting of operational efficiency. Efficiency would require larger units, while private sector investment would assist the investment problem. As one civil engineering specialist in these matters observed, the environmentally sensitive 1980s have given way to the economically sensitive 1990s (Fleming, 1992). The report then set out eight options for consideration.

- Place the services with the new unitary authorities
- Create joint boards of the new authorities
- A lead authority structure
- Create new water authorities
- Create a national water authority
- Joint local authority/private sector schemes
- One or more public limited companies
- Franchising.

Not for the first time, the objectives of securing investment, promoting efficiency and ensuring accountability within a reformed system would be bound to conflict. Public opinion in Scotland remained hostile to a privatisation agenda, a view voiced by leading local government Conservatives. This led the Accounts Commission to conclude that:

> because there is a strong public perception in Scotland that water is not a commercial commodity, an arrangement which involves the public sector in a meaningful way in partnership with the private sector is more likely to command general public support.
> (Accounts Commission, 1993b, p. 5)

Responses to the White Paper showed 94 per cent in favour of retaining public control and 1 per cent voting for privatisation (Black, 1994). At 4834 the scale of response was almost double that for local government reform itself. The government acknowledged this lack of consent to privatisation, and proposed (Scottish Office, 1993a) to create three public water authorities, which would be able to involve private investment. Labour claimed its campaign had halted privatisation, but later shifted its view that the settlement was, like that in England in 1974, an interim one on the road to privatisation. The government clearly showed a concern for sensitive Scottish opinion over privatisation, although public opinion in the main favours the status quo rather than water authorities.

The case for water and sewerage remaining under *public control* is a strong one. To begin with, the professional expertise has been developed within the public sector. Fleming argued that large public limited companies do not have a well-established track record in managing a water and sewerage service, hence a public flotation would have to buy the existing staff to run the company. He sees loyalty to shareholders as conflicting with public health objectives. Moreover, water supply and sewerage disposal would inevitably be monopolies, as scale dictates only three or four companies for reasons of viability. Privatisation would restrict provision in rural areas, and lead to higher charges for consumers (Fleming, 1992, p. 3). Similar concerns were expressed by the Accounts Commission:

> It would not be difficult to take the view that the shareholders' interest has been given particular importance and that the generation of asset and financial resources has featured with undue prominence in the activities of some of the English water companies. (Accounts Commission, 1993b, p. 4)

It was however attracted to the potential of purchasing which left the determination of policies and resource allocation within the local democratic framework.

The distinctive position of water needs to be considered at this point. It is already wholly financed by local taxpayers, although they do not pay in relation to consumption:

> For 1992–3, the estimated cost of providing water and sewerage services in Scotland is £445 million. After allowing for factors such as other income including trade effluent charges the costs to be met amount to £392m.; £210m. for water from charges and rates levied on consumers, and £182m. for sewerage from domestic rates and local authorities' general funds. (Scottish Office, 1992, p. 7)

This consolidated into an average cost per household of £102, well below the English average of £170. The report notes the poor condition of much of the physical infrastructure, and the need for investment. As Black (1994) has observed:

> the absolute cost to the user is likely to be higher under a system based on borrowing from private sources of capital because interest rates will be less favourable to the water agency. Moreover, this does not take into account the dividend expectations of shareholders and remuneration expenditure of top managers, a major consumer grievance in the south.   (p. 31)

Privatisation would therefore be more costly and more difficult to control than public provision, while being politically unacceptable.

Arguments about whether water and sewerage should be a local government service are more complex, and rarely sensibly articulated. Election is assumed to deliver accountability, with little consideration of the *alternatives* for accountability in the public debate.

Autonomy and accountability are twin bedfellows, and the essence of a local government service is policy autonomy, so that members can be accountable for the decisions they take. Increasingly, as we have seen, water and sewerage services are delivered to meet standards set in London and Brussels, and water and sewerage are regarded as national public services. In that context, the government's proposals for appointed water authorities accountable to the Secretary of State, within a framework of a strategic plan, recognises that political power is not exercised locally. Water and sewerage seldom encourage political disagreement. Although they raise sensitive environmental issues, these are not issues of local political choice. The government's proposals recognise that the policy and resource framework under which water authorities would operate is not driven by local factors. Black (1994) argues that this is an attenuated form of accountability, but all forms of political accountability are attenuated, given the range of powers and the limitations of democratic control.

It must be acknowledged, however, that this reform is necessitated by local government restructuring, not by the needs of the services. This point was put nicely by the Accounts Commission:

> the primary difficulty facing the water and sewerage services is that of providing sufficient finance, estimated to be £5 billions, to comply with a variety of European Community directives and the assurance of a long-term capital investment programme which would provide the required range and quality of facilities into the future. The need

is therefore one of investment management and accountability rather than the identification of structural deficiencies in the existing arrangements. Had it not been for the prospect of a major reorganisation in Scottish local authorities the question would have to be asked as to the need for the various proposed options to be considered at all. (Accounts Commission, 1993b, p. 3)

Although water and sewerage has been a politically sensitive issue, it has not as yet excited the passions in the public as did the poll tax. The government's proposals appear workable, and if water continues to flow through the taps after changeover, and the government manages the cash consequences of new investment carefully, then a public revolt can be avoided. Water and sewerage are essential public services, which need public regulation. However, the Scottish public remain wary of the government's proposals, and their implementation will need to be carefully handled indeed.

The problem of transferring services

COSLA's strategy of non-co-operation has muddied the waters in terms of arguments over the problems of transferring service responsibilities to the new authorities. It has been argued that the timetable is unrealistic, but this is capable of political interpretation as part of the wider strategy to prevent implementation of the reforms. It is also the case that some authorities support this line within COSLA, while offering a different view in their own right. This has promoted scepticism within government about the realism of the timetabling protests:

> The fact is that the timetable for reorganisation, which envisages elections to the shadow authorities on 6 April 1995, with the new authorities assuming responsibility a year later, is almost identical to that which applied for the last reorganisation in 1975. Much has changed since then, of course, but few would argue with the view that the authorities of to-day are, by and large, in a much greater state of efficiency and organisation than that of many of their predecessors.
>
> Once again, plenty of authorities are prepared to tell us that they can achieve the present timetable. The messages of gloom come from those which are facing their own demise. (Stewart, A., 1994, p. 18)

The Minister's view that the new authorities are efficiently organised compared with their predecessors is hard to square with the government's conventional critique of the new system as bureaucratic and inefficient! That said, his views need more qualification. First, the situation today *is* more complex than in 1975. Although the trend now, as then, is to *fewer* authorities, the last reorganisation was in the main occupied with *merging* service departments. In 1996, the single biggest organisational problem will be the need to *disaggregate* regional services in Central, Grampian, Lothian, Strathclyde and Tayside. As regional services account for some 85 per cent of local expenditure, this is not insignificant.

Secondly, though it is true that the loudest protests are from authorities being broken up, *it is those very authorities which have the experience of managing the major local government services*. Arguments that the timetable is manageable tend to come from those districts whose boundaries will form the basis of the new authorities, but whose service responsibilities, and hence experience, are very limited. There clearly is an issue of concern here which should not be dismissed in a peremptory fashion. Thirdly, at the last reorganisation, the added complication of CCT did not exist: staff were transferred and budgets revised accordingly. This time, the new councils will inherit contractual obligations, and some of these will require disaggregation. Finally, there is the requirement on authorities to comply with the Acquired Rights Directive of the EC and the Transfer of Undertakings (TUPE) Regulations in the UK. The implications of these complexities need consideration.

Local authorities are labour-intensive: staff costs form the largest single element of costs, and almost half of total costs. In 1975, almost all staff transferred to the new authorities. This time, the government has been more explicit in identifying job loss as a means of securing financial savings, although the scale of savings anticipated has been considerably reduced. It is clearly the case that the vast majority of local authority staff will simply transfer to the new authorities. Government policy is that automatic transfer should apply in most cases, with advice from the Staff Commission as to precisely *which* staff this applies to. The issue was put recently in debate in the House of Lords by Lord Rodger of Earlferry:

The vast majority of those employed in local government will be transferred. Plainly a school which comprises a number of teachers of say French or Science on 31 March 1996 will need the same teachers on the following day, so the teachers will transfer. As I have said, the vast majority of staff will transfer, so we are talking about a relatively small number of people who will not transfer. (*Hansard*, 13 July 1994, para. 1899).

The Staff Commission in Scotland has yet to address these issues at the time of writing. Its English counterpart suggests that automatic transfer should apply to manual and craft workers, to other staff whose work involves service provision direct to the public and specific locations, and to administrative and managerial staff who are wholly employed in relation to those other staff who themselves are to be transferred.

The problem areas will be in central services and in specialist services in areas of education and social work, which function on a region-wide basis. This issue has been addressed in a finance context by a senior finance officer in Strathclyde. Scholes (1994) argued that there will be major problems in disaggregating this and other regional central services. The difficulty in staffing terms flows from the rationalisation which has occurred since 1975, in relation to the home location of staff in contrast with the office location of the new authorities:

The regional revenue staff have tended over the 20 or so years since the last reorganisation to be recruited from the local area of the sub-regional offices. There are very few staff now travelling to revenues work from other centres of population which might become the HQs of new authorities. There will be a reluctance for staff to move to new authorities not based in sub-regional locations and, even with transfer costs and excess Council costs paid, certain new authorities would experience difficulty in obtaining the higher level staff to support their revenue activity and, in due course, in retaining lower-level revenue staff since it is likely that they will start to search for jobs close to home. (Scholes, 1994, p. 3)

Scholes also queried the availability of suitable accommodation for information technology purposes, and argued for temporary arrangements to permit continuity of tax collection, by retaining staff in these sub-regional offices as outposted staff of the new authorities. He also foresaw difficulties in transferring systems from mainframe computers to PCs. The problem is compounded when staff in central services departments deal with functions which will be removed from direct council authority control, such as police, fire, water and sewerage. Such staff include vehicle mechanics, caterers, cleaners, or accountants, many of whom will function on a *contract* basis. Here too, making new arrangements for information technology will be a major consideration. These are central to daily operations.

If we turn our attention to contracted services, the difficulties are already being recognised. The government has published a consultative paper setting out the issues, as CCT is due to be extended. Consideration of the issue led to recognition that the

> scale of calls on the management resources of an authority in the period immediately surrounding local government reorganisation led Ministers to announce a deferment of the extension of CCT and to announce that CCT for existing services would also be suspended for a period.   (Scottish Office, 1994, para. 5)

The deferment arrangements give authorities 18–24 months to implement the extension of CCT, but this has been criticised by authorities as unrealistic. The structural changes create diverse problems for authorities, who will

> inherit a variety of arrangements made by their predecessors. These may in some cases be contiguous with the new boundaries and in other cases will reflect previous administrative arrangements. Other authorities will inherit a number of agreements made by different authorities for the same service.   (Scottish Office, 1991b, para. 29)

The paper goes on to argue that elements of the existing arrangements may be inappropriate to the successor authorities and identifies four options for handling such arrangements.

- a local authority;
- a joint committee;
- division of the agreement; or
- new tenders or external provision.

The final two arrangements could be used where large regional DSOs *are not* easily broken up into the constituent parts, and provide for some continuity until an orderly change can be effected. But these can only be short-term arrangements. For such staff, uncertainty over their future will remain.

Finally, we turn to the issue of TUPE. Both Unison and COSLA favour an arrangement whereby *all* staff transfer to the new authorities on day one, and rationalisation then takes place. This is resisted by the government, for quite sensible reasons. TUPE provides that where an 'undertaking' or part of one, is transferred from one legal firm to another, the employees' contracts of employment, which would otherwise be terminated by the transfer, will continue as if made between the new employer and employee. Dismissal of an employee by reason only of the transfer is treated as unfair dismissal. The employers retain the right to dismiss staff for an 'economic, technical or organisational' reason. An undertaking is regarded as an economic entity capable of operating as a going concern and which retains its identity when transferred.

Unison has campaigned for assurances from government and council that 'TUPE applies' to reorganisation. This implies that councils have some choice in the matter whereas it is a matter of *law*. TUPE does apply, but interpretation of how it applies can only be determined in court. Some interpretation of it may assist the implementation process, but is is not clear how transferring *all* staff would do so if rationalisation took place after reorganisation. TUPE does not appear to apply in *all* cases, and certainly not in the same way in all authorities.

There are broadly three new types of authority – based in an existing *regional* boundary; an existing *district* boundary; or a *new* boundary, usually involving two or more existing districts. In the first of these, it is arguable that operational services of the existing regions are subject to TUPE, as the job and area of authority has not changed. What if, however, the new authority decides to merge social work and housing ? The same arguments could be made of district services in the second category. In the third category, it seems likely that only a subdivision of the existing regional services, or operational aspects of district services, would be subject to TUPE. Elias (1994) considers that it is not possible to state categorically whether TUPE will apply in the context of reorganisation:

> it is likely to do so where the functions of an authority are trans-
> ferred to a new body, even although the identity of the transferor
> becomes merged into the new body. The position is more uncertain
> where an authority's functions are divided between successor autho-
> rities, but even then I suspect that, adopting a robust approach,

TUPE would apply. Even if it does not apply to the whole of the operation transferred, it is likely to apply to particular activities which can be seen as part of the undertaking in their own right. (Elias, 1994, p. 27)

Depending on the geographic circumstances therefore, TUPE could apply to an entire service such as education, or simply to each of its schools on an individual basis. Likewise, it could apply to all social work staff, or only to those in operational roles in residential homes, home helps, and so on. The expectation is that the majority of staff will transfer, and the remaining posts will be filled by competition. Those who have not obtained a post by 31 March 1996 will be declared redundant under the legislation and eligible for compensation. Given the authorities' right to rationalise, it is not at all clear what benefit wholesale transfer would bring to such affected staff.

In the government's view, it is for the new authorities to determine appropriate staffing levels and structure; transferring all staff would simply postpone the decisions on rationalisation:

Would it not be better to ensure that the shadow authorities themselves have to consider the staffing that will be appropriate for the new authorities when they take over in April 1996. Would it not be better to decide that as early as possible and those who are going to transfer will know as early as possible what package is available to them and can make their arrangements accordingly. (*Hansard*, 13 July 1994, para. 1900)

COSLA argues that wholesale transfer may reduce the scale of appeals made under TUPE. It may, but to whose benefit? It may be preferable for staff faced with redundancy to have the option of a challenge in court. It is clear that TUPE does not apply to all staff, and will vary between areas. Reliance on TUPE will not bring equity: that still remains the realm of public policy. However, it is also clear that the incidence of complicating factors in this reorganisation is greater than last time, and as a result, implementation will be more difficult.

The problem of controlling costs

The potential of a single-tier system to deliver efficiency gains through financial savings was a dominant theme early in the reform process, but one which has declined in prominence as the questionable realism of the financial assumptions was widely recognised. Indeed, the local government minister, Allan Stewart, was at pains to stress the limited job loss likely to result from reorganisation, and hence the limited savings:

> Let me lay the misinformed debate on costs to rest first of all. The government has estimated – on the basis of the work done by Touche Ross and of comments made about that work – that the transitional costs of reorganisation will be in the order of £120m–£191m over 15 years, and that annuals saving of *up to* [my emphasis] £53m will accrue . . .

but

> It is worth making the point, however, that no exact estimate will ever be possible. Ultimately, the actual costs and savings will be determined by decisions taken by individual authorities themselves. (Stewart, 1994, p. 18)

These estimates have been challenged by COSLA, but this has been weakened by authorities predicting 'greater' savings if they were the 'new' authority. All such claims are based on assumptions, and as good as these.

There are, however, two related points that need consideration. The first of these is that all authorities are required to produce schemes of administrative decentralisation to allow control of service delivery to be as local as possible. This is seen as a way of making service delivery more responsive and sensitive to the public. Whatever the merits of that argument, it is clear that the need for decentralisation could have cost implications, as the experience of decentralisation in health or education has shown. The argument for larger authorities is that such authorities provide economies of scale in administration. These have been well summarised in a recent paper by Boyne *et al.* (1994):

> The basic features of the model are that fragmentation of units is bad and concentration of functions is good. This implies that units should be large in order to reap economies of scale in service provision. According to the managerial model, the existence of a large number of small units causes diseconomies of scale, for example, because of the duplication of administrative overheads –

large units, by contrast, can spread these 'fixed costs' over higher levels of service production and are therefore more efficient.   (p. 25)

The government's new map provides for two distinctive trends. In the rural regions and Fife, the larger units survive and the smaller units are disbanded, providing the potential for economies of scale in administration. In the larger regions, which account for most of the Scottish population, the larger units are broken up, removing the potential for administrative savings. This has been recognised by most professional organisations in their responses to the consultation papers, but, as Boyne *et al.* note 'despite this comprehensive drubbing of the validity arguments for greater administrative efficiency, the government clings to its view that the new system will be cheaper to run' (ibid., p. 36).

The realism of the financial modelling exercise remains in doubt to the practical men who will manage the new system. Scholes (1994) argued that the splitting up of large regions into smaller unitary authorities will increase the numbers of staff overall, and also the number of higher graded staff. The economies of scale which derive from having only one system and one set of policies will be lost, as new administrative hierarchies are required. Once a decentralised system is superimposed upon this – an aspect of reform not considered in the financial predictions made by the government – then the prospects for financial savings appear to be diminished.

The second aspect of concern is the costs of service provision. The government has recognised the validity of scale arguments in the context of service delivery costs in the past, when authorities were self-sufficient providers. The decrease of direct service provision has diminished the relevance of these arguments, in the government's view. We have shown, however, that the dominant municipal provision role will remain, and that it is unwise to assume no change in service delivery costs as a result. We can explore this further.

Past reorganisations have taken the benefits of scale as given, although the evidence has often been regarded as contradictory. One recent review of the literature in this field concluded that population size has no consistent impact on costs. (Travers *et al.*, 1993). There are, however, methodological problems in most attempts to examine the relationship between population size and efficiency. The conventional approach is to correlate size with costs via regression analysis, which would identify a linear relationship. This has two problems. First, economies of scale arguments relate to *unit costs*, not *total* costs.

Authorities' total spending is a reflection of their unit costs and the *volume* of provision. Disaggregating data into unit costs is a difficult task, because of the problems of identifying a unit of service. As we have seen, the concept of standard service is central to the objectives of needs assessment, yet is left undefined because of the conceptual problems. What is a unit of service in the public library service? Is it simply the *cost* of borrowing books, for example? This can vary with controls on the number of books one is permitted to borrow at any time, the size of the population, the numbers and type of service points, and so on. The existence or non-existence of a correlation with total spending is not of itself evidence of size effect, or the absence of one. It needs to be related to outputs and usage (Midwinter and McVicar, 1993). The plausibility of the statistical findings need to be carefully considered.

This approach was used by Travers *et al.* (1993). They examined development control, education and fire costs. The first of these examines variations between small authorities and the last of these examines variations between large authorities, as only one fire authority has a population of less than 200 000. The lack of consistent evidence is an academic issue, not a policy one. What matters in the reorganisation context is the findings on specific services, and the potential impact of disaggregating large regional authorities (or counties in the English context). The absence of statistical evidence in the case of district services, provided by authorities with small populations, is of little direct relevance to the costs issue. The key services in a Scottish context are education, social work, and roads and transport.

Here, the Rowntree evidence has policy relevance. The researchers conclude that there is

> an apparent tendency for smaller authorities to have somewhat higher expenditure levels than large ones. This apparent link is borne out by the correlation co-efficient (0.398). The result is statistically significant. The trend for larger authorities to spend less per pupil than smaller ones is also apparent when authorities are grouped to take account of the social and economic backgrounds of children. (Travers *et al.*, 1993, p. 51)

The researchers have attempted to take some account of variations in need. Moreover, past studies show that central concern for staffing standards in schools has a significant effect on levels of provision, leading to much less variation in spending than is found in some discretionary services such as leisure and recreation (Midwinter and Page, 1981). When we examine the cost pattern of the smallest (< 200 000) English authorities in the Rowntree study, we find they spend on average 11 per cent *above* the average, whereas the largest (1 million plus) spend 8 per cent *below* the average. This is not to argue that size is the dominant cause of expenditure differences. Differences in need and policy play a part (Elcock *et al.*, 1989). There is, however, enough evidence to suggest the possibility of a scale effect, which could add to costs when the large education authorities are disaggregated. The government is somewhat rash to discount the possibility of cost changes in such services. A similar pattern can be found in social work services (Midwinter and McGarvey, 1994).

The prospect remains, therefore, that costs will rise at reorganisation. This will bring trickly fiscal problems for the government. If they set capping levels too tightly, then services will be squeezed, and reorganisation will be blamed. If they set grant levels too tightly, then local taxes will rise, and reorganisation will be blamed. This will discredit the system in its infancy. It will be a nice political judgement, and the practice of assuming 'fairy gold' efficiency savings in the grant settlement each year only compounds the uncertainty.

Conclusions

This final chapter has identified a number of key political problems for the government in implementing its reforms. It still has to convince a sceptical public that there are real benefits to be gained from reform of structures in general, and water in particular. Scepticism that reform is being pursued for narrow partisan advantage remains commonplace.

That scepticism will be compounded if a realistic approach is not adopted to the transfer of responsibilities, to avoid service delivery problems in the early stages. Transferring schools, residential homes, or swimming baths, will be relatively unproblematic; but information technology, central support services, or specialist services are another matter, for which some temporary joint arrangements may be necessary in the period of transition.

Finally, the avoidance of rising costs will require careful fiscal management. In the current system, some 90 per cent of local income is centrally controlled. Any shortfall caused by inadequate grant or rising service costs will fall visibly on local taxpayers. This is not a time for rash provision of efficiency savings based on guesswork. The absence of expenditure data for the new authorities will of itself make the client group system impossible to apply for at least three years, and a way of providing stability of grant income will be needed in any temporary needs assessment system. In local government finance, the prospect of unforeseen difficulties becoming fiscal problems in a system of minimal autonomy is ever present.

The case for reform is not a good one. No clear benefits are on offer. The prospect of higher costs and lower services remains a possibility. The main criticism of the government is not that their proposals are unattainable, for in the technical sense the reform can be effected, albeit with new problems. It is that it is not clear that any benefit to the Scottish public will materialise, and that a further period of turbulence in local government is certain. Given the failure of the poll tax in the 1980s, and the lessons it brought in terms of making policy without consensus and on the basis of little analysis, a more considered approach would have been beneficial. Rather a period of further uncertainty, in which a further reorganisation occurs, either because of the lack of viability of small authorities, or as part of a devolution package, is the order of the day.

References

ACCOUNTS COMMISSION (1988) *Auditing Guideline – Value-for-Money* (Edinburgh: Accounts Commission)
—— (1991a) *Focus on Value-for-Money*, June issue (Edinburgh).
—— (1991b) *Focus on Value-for-Money*, October issue (Edinburgh).
—— (1992) *Focus on Value-for-Money*, November issue (Edinburgh).
—— (1993a) *Focus on Value-for-Money*, March issue (Edinburgh).
—— (1993b) *Water and Sewerage in Scotland: Investing in our Future* (Edinburgh: Accounts Commission).
ADAM SMITH INSTITUTE (1989) *Shedding a Tier* (London: ASI).
ADLER, M., A. PETCH and J. TWEEDIE (1987) 'The Origins and Impact of the Parents Charter' in *The Scottish Government Yearbook, 1987* (Edinburgh: University of Edinburgh).
ALEXANDER, A. (1982a) *The Politics of Local Government in the United Kingdom* (London: Longman).
—— (1982b) *Local Government in Britain since Reorganisation* (London: George Allen & Unwin).
—— (1992) 'Constitutional Stalemate and Institutional Reform: Reforming Scottish Local Government', *Scottish Affairs*, no. 1 (Autumn) pp. 55–65.
ALEXANDER, D. (1985) Public Sector Housing in Scotland: Trends and Prospects', in *The Scottish Government Yearbook, 1985* (Edinburgh: University of Edinburgh).
ASCHER, K. (1987) *The Politics of Privatisation* (Basingstoke: Macmillan Education).
AUDIT COMMISSION (1984) *The Impact of Local Authorities' Economy, Efficiency and Effectiveness of the Block Grant Distribution System* (London: HMSO).
AUDIT COMMISSION (1991) *Response to the Government's Consultation Paper – a New Tax for Local Government* (London: Audit Commission).
BAILEY, S. (1988) 'The Economics of Public Library Charities', in *New Library World*, Nov., pp. 203–65.
—— (1990) 'Implementing Local Public Choice: The Community Charge', in Tal Younis (ed.), *Implementation in Public Policy*.
—— (1992) 'Public Choice Theory and the Reform of Local Government in Britain: from Government to Governance', Department of Economics, Glasgow Polytechnic. Discussion Paper no. 16.
—— (1993) 'Public Choice Theory and the Reform of Local Government in Britain', *Public Policy and Administration*, vol. 8, no. 2 (Summer) pp. 7–24.
BARNETT, R. and C. KNOX (1992) 'Accountability and Local Budgetary Policy', *Policy and Politics*, vol. 20, no. 4, pp. 265–76).
BEALE, V. and C. POLLIT (1994) 'Charters at the Grass Roots: A First Report'. (forthcoming).

BLACK, S. (1993) 'CCT in Scottish Local Government', *Scottish Affairs*, no. 3 (Spring) pp. 188–134.
—— (1994) 'What's Happening to the Water and Sewerage Services in Scotland', *Scottish Affairs*, no. 6 (Winter) pp. 25–35.
BLOCH, A. and P. JOHN (1991) *Attitudes to Local Government – A Survey of Electors* (York: Joseph Rowntree Foundation).
BONNER, S. and J. McCONNEL (1993) 'On a quest for quality', in G. W. Jones (eds), *Local Government: The Management Agenda* (London: ICSA).
BOYNE, G. (1992) 'The Reform of Local Government in Wales: A Critique of the Case for Unitary Authorities', *Public Money and Management*, Jul./Sept., pp. 1–4.
BOYNE, G., G. JORDAN and M. McVICAR (1994) 'Local Government Reorganisation – the Effects of Structural Change', Working Paper no. 4, Joseph Rowntree Study, University of Aberdeen.
BRUCE, A. and G. LEE (1982) 'Local Election Campaigns', *Political Studies*, 30: 2, pp. 247–61.
BULPITT, J. (1983) *Territory and Power in the United Kingdom: An Interpretation* (Manchester: MUP).
—— (1989) 'Walking Back to Happiness?, Conservative Party Governments and Elected Local Authorities in the 1980s', in C. Crouch and D. Maynard (eds), *The New Centralism: Britain Out of Step in Europe* (Oxford: Basil Blackwell).
BUTCHER, H., I. LAW, R. LEACH and M. MULLARD (1990) *Local Government and Thatcherism* (London: Routledge).
BUTT, H. and B. PALMER (1985) *Value-for-Money in the Public Sector – The Decision-Makers' Guide* (Oxford: Basil Blackwell).
CARMICHAEL, P. (1992) 'Is Scotland Different? Local Government Policy under Mrs Thatcher', *Local Government Policy Making*, vol. 18, no. 5, pp. 25–33.
CARTER, N. (1988) 'Measuring Government Performance', *Political Quarterly*, vol. 59, 3 pp. 369–75.
—— (1991) 'Learning to Measure Performance: The Use of Indicators in Organizations', *Public Administration*, vol. 69 (Spring) pp. 85–101.
CLARK, G (1984) 'A Theory of Local Autonomy', *Annals of the Association of American Geographies*, vol. 74, pp. 195–208.
CLARKE, M. and J. D. STEWART (1988) *The Enabling Council* (Luton: LGTB).
—— (1991) *Choices for Local Government* (Harlow: Longman).
COCHRANE, A. (1991) 'The Changing State of Local Government: Restructuring for the 1990s', *Public Administration*, vol. 69 (Autumn) pp. 281–302.
—— (1993) 'Whatever Happened to Local Government (Buckingham: OUP).
COHEN, B. (1991) 'Developing Childcare Services in Scotland: Whose Responsibility?', in A. Brown and D. McCrone (eds), *The Scottish Government Yearbook 1991*, pp. 217–28 (Edinburgh: Unit for the Study of Government in Scotland).
COMELY, D. (1990) *The Future for Community Care in Scotland* (Glasgow: Department of Housing, City of Glasgow District Council).

COMMITTEE OF INQUIRY (1986) *Report into the Pay and Conditions of Service of School Teachers in Scotland* (Edinburgh: HMSO; Cmnd 9898) (The Main Report).

COMMON, R., N. FLYNN and E. MELLOR (1993) *Public Services: Competitive and Decentralisation* (Oxford: Butterworth–Heinemann).

COSLA (1988) CCT Bulletin no. 1, March (Edinburgh: COSLA).

—— (1990) 'Local Authority Costs of Community Care Developments – Survey of Likely Infrastructure Costs' (Report) (Edinburgh: COSLA).

—— (1992) 'Response to Scottish Office Environment Department Consultation Paper – CCT for Housing Management in Scotland' (Report) (Edinburgh: COSLA).

—— (1993) 'The Cost of Restructuring Local Government in Scotland' (Edinburgh: COSLA).

CREWE, I. (1989) 'Values! The Crusade that Failed' in D. Kavanagh and A. Seldon (eds), *The Thatcher Effect: A Decade of Change* (Oxford: Clarendon Press).

CROUCH, C. and D. MAYNARD (1989) *The New Centralism: Britain Out of Step with Europe?* (Oxford: Basil Blackwell).

CSL (1993) 'Sparsity Indicators for GAE Assessments', Report prepared for the Scottish Office.

DAVIES, H. (1988) 'New Directors in Local Accountability: Can the People be Trusted?', *Public Money and Management* (Spring/Summer) pp. 57–60.

DAWSON, D. (1983) 'Financial Incentives for Change', in K. Young (ed.), *National Interested and Local Government* (London: Policy Studies Institute).

DEARLOVE, J. (1979) *The Reorganisation of British Local Government* (Cambridge University Press, Cambridge).

DOE (1991) 'A New Tax for Local Government – A Consultation Paper', April (London: HMSO).

DOWNS, G. W. and P. D. LARKEY (1986) *The Search for Government Efficiency* (Philadelphia: Temple).

DRUCKER, P. (1968) *The Age of Discontinuity* (New York: Harper Torchbooks).

DUNLEAVY, P. (1979) *Urban Political Analysis* (Basingstoke: Macmillan).

—— (1986) 'Explaining The Privatisation Boom: Public Choice Versus Radical Explanation', *Public Administration*, vol. 64, no. 1, pp. 13–34.

ELCOCK, H., G. JORDAN and A. MIDWINTER (1989) *Budgeting in Local Government: Managing the Margins* (Harlow: Longman).

ELIAS, P. (1994) 'Application of 16 Transfer of Undertakings (Protection of Employment) Regulations 1981 to Local Government Reorganisation', Advice prepared for the Local Government Management Branch.

ENGLISH, J. (ed.) (1988) *Social Services in Scotland* (Edinburgh: Scottish Academic Press).

ENNALS, K. and J. O'BRIEN (1990) 'The Enabling Role of Local Authorities', Research Report no. 1 (London: KPMM).

FLEMING, G. (1992) 'The Future Water and Sewerage in Scotland – Response to the Consultation Document' (Glasgow: University of Strathclyde).

FLYNN, N. (1988) 'A Consumer–Oriented Culture', *Public Money and Management* (Spring/Summer) pp. 27–31.

FORSYTH, M. (1980) *Reservicing Britain* (London: Adam Smith Institute).

FRASER, LORD P. (1992) 'Scotland in Britain', The Paradox Shaping Our Identity (Address to the Conservative Political Centre Annual Summer School).
—— 'The Pros and Cons of School Opting Out', *Scotsman*, 29 Sep. 1993, p. 20.
FRY, M. (1987) *Patronage and Principle: A Political History of Modern Scotland* (Aberdeen: Aberdeen University Press).
GALBRAITH, K. (1973) *Economics and the Public Purpose* (New York: NAL Penguin).
GAMBLE, A. (1984) *The Free Economy and the Strong State* (London: Macmillan).
GIBSON, J. (1987) 'The Reform of British Local Government Finance: the limits of local accountability', *Policy and Politics*, vol. 15, pp. 167–74.
GILMOUR, I. (1978) *Inside Right* (London: Quartet Books).
GOODIN, R. (1982) 'Rational Politicians and Rational Bureaucrats in Washington and Whitehall', *Public Administration*, vol. 60, no. 1 pp. 23–92.
GOODSELL, C. T. (1990) *The Case for Bureaucracy* (New Jersey: Cheltenham House Publication).
GREENWOOD, R. and J. STEWART (1974) *Corporate Planning in English Local Government 1967–73* (London: Charles Knight).
GRIFFITHS REPORT (1988) *Community Care: Agenda for Action* (London: HMSO).
GYFORD, J. (1991) *Citizens, Consumers and Councils* (London: Macmillan)..
HAMBLETON, R. and P. HOGGET (1990) *Decentralisation and Democracy: Localising Public Services*, Occasional Paper no. 28 (School for Advanced Urban Studies, Bristol).
HARRISON, A. (1989) *The Control of Public Expenditure* (Transaction Books, Oxford).
HEALD, D. (1994) 'Territorial Public Expenditure in the United Kingdom', *Public Administration*, vol. 72, pp. 147–75.
HEATH, A., R. JOWELL and J. CURTICE (1985) *How Britain Votes* (Oxford: Pergamon Press).
HENDERSON-STEWART, D. (1988) 'Performance Measurement and Review in Local Government', in M. Cave, M. Kogan and R. Smith, *Output and Performance Measurement in Government* (Jessica Kingsley, London).
HENNEY, A. (1984) *Inside Local Government: A Case in Radical Reform* (London: Sinclair Browne).
HILL, D. (1974) *Democratic Theory and Local Government* (London: Allen & Unwin).
HM TREASURY (1982) *Financial Management in Government Departments* (HMSO, London: Cmnd 9058).
—— (1986) *Output and Performance Measurement in Central Government: Progress in Departments* (Working Paper no. 38) (HMSO, London).
HOLLIDAY, I. (1993) 'Scottish Limits to Thatcherism', *Political Quarterly*, vol. 64, pp. 448–59.
HOLTHAM, C. and J. STEWART (1981) *Value-for-Money – A Framework for Action* (Inlogov, Birmingham).
HOOD, C. (1976) *The Limits of Administration* (London: Wiley).
—— (1991) 'A Public Management for All Seasons?', *Public Administration* (Spring) vol. 69, pp. 3–20.

HUNTER, D. J. and G. WISTOW (1988) 'The Scottish Difference: Policy and Practice in Community Care', in *The Scottish Government Yearbook 1988* (Edinburgh: Unit for the Study of Government in Scotland).

INSTITUTE OF HOUSING (1993) *Observations on The Scottish Office Environment Department Housing*, Consultation Paper (Edinburgh).

JACKSON, P. (1988) 'The Management of Performance in the Public Sector', *Public Money and Management* (Winter) pp. 11–16.

—— (1989) *The Political Economy of Bureaucracy* (Oxford: Philip Allen).

JONES, B. and M. KEATING (1988) 'Beyond the Doomsday Scenario: Governing Scotland and Wales in the 1980s', *Strathclyde Papers on Government and Politics*, no. 58 (Glasgow: University of Strathclyde).

JONES, G. W. (1977) *Responsibility in Government* (London: London School of Economics).

—— (1992) 'The Search for Local Accountability', in S. Leach (ed.), *Strengthening Local Government in the 1990s* (Essex: Longman).

JONES, G. W. and J. D. STEWART (1983) *The Case for Local Government* (London: Allen & Unwin).

JONES, R. and M. PENDLEBURY (1984) *Public Sector Accounting* (Pitman Publishing, London).

JUDGE, D. (1993) *The Parliamentary State* (London: Sage).

KAVANAGH, P. (1987) *Thatcherism and British Politics: The End of Consensus?*, (Oxford: OUP)

KEATING, M. and A. MIDWINTER (1993) 'The Politics of Local Fiscal Equalisation in Britain and France', Paper presented to the Urban Affairs Association Conference, Indianapolis, April.

KERLEY, R. (1992) 'Devolution and Local Government: Some Lessons from the Scottish Experience', *Public Policy and Administration*, vol. 7, no. 1 (Spring) pp. 21–30.

KERLEY, R. and D. WYNN (1990) 'Competitive Tendering: The Contracted Service Provision in Scottish Local Authorities SLAMC Papers in Local Government 1/90' (Glasgow: University of Strathclyde).

KING, A. (1975) *Why is Britain Becoming More Difficult to Govern* (London: BBC Publishing).

KING, D. (1988) *The New Right: Politics, Markets and Citizenship* (Basingstoke: Macmillan Education).

KOGAN, M. (1973) 'Observations on Niskanen', in *Bureaucracy: Servant or Master?* (London: IEA).

LANG, I. (1992) 'Bringing the Union Alive', Address to the Monday Club, Brighton.

LANG, I. (1994) The 1994 Swinton Lecture.

LAWSON, N. (1981) *The New Conservatism* (London: Centre for Policy Studies).

LAYFIELD (1976) Report of the Committee of Inquiry into Local Government Finance (London: HMSO).

LEACH, S. (1982) 'In Defence of the Rational Model', in Leach and Stewart (eds), *Approaches in Public Policy* (London: Allen & Unwin).

LEACH, S., H. DAVIS, C. GAME and C. SKELCHER (1992) *After Abolition* (Birmingham: INLOGOV).

LE GRAND, J. (1990) *Quasi Markets and Social Policy*, Studies in Decentralisation and Quasi Markets, no. 1 (Bristol: School for Advanced Urban Studies).

LETWYN, S. (1992) The Anatomy of Thatcherism (London: Fontana).

LINDBLOM, C. (1959) 'The Science of Muddling Through', *Public Administration Review*, 19 (Spring) pp. 79–88.

LOCAL GOVERNMENT MANAGEMENT BOARD (1994) *Fitness for Purpose* (Luton: LGMB).

LOCAL GOVERNMENT INFORMATION UNIT (1992) 'Council Tax: Local Government Finance Act 1992', *Special Briefing*, no. 41.

McLENNAN, D. (1989) 'Municipal Housing in Scotland: The Long Goodbye', in *The Scottish Government Yearbook 1989* (Edinburgh: University of Edinburgh).

MAJOR, J. (1992) *Scotland in the United Kingdom* (London: Conservative Political Centre).

MACPHERSON, A. (1989) 'Social and Political Aspects of the Devolved Management of Scottish Secondary Schools', *Scottish Educational Review*, vol. 21 (2), pp. 87–100.

MARTLEW, C. (1988) *Local Democracy in Practice* (Aldershot: Avebury).

McCRONE, D. (1993) *Understanding Scotland: The Sociology of a Stateless Nation* (London: Routledge).

McCRONE, D., A. BROWN and L. PATERSON (1992) *The Structure of Local Government in Scotland: An Analysis of Submissions to The Scottish Office, Consultation Paper* (Edinburgh: Edinburgh University).

McVICAR, M., A. G. JORDAN and G. BOYNE (1994) 'Ships in the Night: Scottish Political Parties and Local Government Reform', *Scottish Affairs*, vol. 9 (Autumn) pp. 80–96.

MIDWINTER, A. (1984) *The Politics of Local Spending* (Edinburgh: Mainstream).

—— (1990) 'A Return to Ratepaying Democracy: The Reform of Local Government Finance in Historical Perspective', *Scottish Economic and Social History*, vol. 10, pp. 61–9.

—— (1993) 'Community, Democracy and Local Government Reform – The Implications for Lothian', Paper prepared for Lothian Regional Council.

MIDWINTER, A., M. KEATING and J. MITCHELL (1991) *Politics and Public Policy in Scotland* (Basingstoke: Macmillan).

MIDWINTER, A., M. KEATING and P. TAYLOR (1983) 'Excessive and Unreasonable: The Politics of the Scottish Hit List', *Political Studies*, Sep.

MIDWINTER, A. and C. MAIR (1987) *Rates Reform: Issues, Arguments and Evidence* (Edinburgh: Mainstream).

MIDWINTER, A., C. MAIR and C. FORD (1987) 'Rating Revaluation Revisited', in D. McCrone (ed.), *The Scottish Government Yearbook, 1987* (Edinburgh: Edinburgh University).

MIDWINTER, A. and N. McGARVEY (1994) 'The Restructuring of Scotland's Education Authorities: Does Size Matter?', *Scottish Educational Review*, vol. 26, no. 2, pp. 110–17.

MIDWINTER, A. and M. McVICAR (1992) 'Public Library Finance: Developments in Scotland', *Library and Information Research Report*, no. 85 (London: The British Library).

—— (1993) 'Population Size and Functional Efficiency in Public Library Authorities: The Statistical Evidence', *Journal of Librarianship and Information Science*, vol. 25, no. 4, December, pp. 187–96.

MIDWINTER, A. and C. MONAGHAN (1991a) *The Planning and Control of Local Authority Capital Expenditure in Scotland* (Glasgow: Chartered Association of Certified Accountants).

—— (1991b) 'The New System of Local Government Finance in Scotland: Principles and Practice', *Public Administration*, vol. 6, no. 3, pp. 345–61.

—— (1993) *From Rates To The Poll Tax: Local Government Finance in the Thatcher Years* (Edinburgh: Edinburgh University Press).

MIDWINTER, A. and E. PAGE (1981) 'Reducing Local Expenditure: The Scottish Experience, 1976–80', in Hood and Wright (eds), *Big Government in Hard Times* (London: Macmillan).

MILLER, W. (1986) *The Local Government Election*, Research vol. 111, Report of the Committee of Inquiry into the Conduct of Local Authority Business (Cmnd 9800: London: HMSO).

—— (1988) *Irrelevant Elections?: The Quality of Local Democracy in Britain* (Oxford: Clarendon Press).

MONTGOMERY, D. (1983) Committee of Inquiry into the Functions and Powers of Islands Councils of Scotland (Edinburgh: HMSO).

MOORE, C. (1991) 'Reflections on the New Local Political Economy: Resignation, Resistance and Reform', *Policy and Politics*, vol. 19, no. 2, pp. 73–80.

MUNN, P. (1992) 'Devoted Management of Schools and FE Colleges: A Victory for the Producer over the Consumer?', in *The Scottish Government Yearbook 1992* (Edinburgh: University of Edinburgh).

NEWTON, K. (1976) *Second City Politics* (London: OUP).

—— (1977) 'Is small really beautiful? Is big really so ugly? Size, effectiveness and democracy in local government', *Political Studies*, pp. 190–206.

—— (1981) *Urban Political Economy* (London: Frances Pinter).

NEWTON, K. and T. KARRAN (1985) *The Politics of Local Expenditure* (Edinburgh: Mainstream).

NISKANEN, W. (1971) *Bureaucracy and Representative Government* (Beverley Hills: Sage).

OSBORNE, D. and T. GAEBLER (1993) *Reinventing Government: How the Entrepreneurial Spirit is Transforming the Public Sector* (New York: Plume).

OSTROM, E. (1983) 'A Public Choice Approach to Metropolitan Institutions: Structure, Incentives and Performance', *Social Science Journal*, 20, pp. 79–96.

PAGE, C. S. (1969) 'Administrative Costs of Local Authorities', Paper prepared for the Wheatley Commission.

PAGE, E. (1978) 'Why should Central-Local Relations in Scotland Be Different to Those in England?', *Public Administration*, Bulletin no. 28, Dec. pp. 51–72.

—— (1989) 'Management Statistics and Performance Indicators in British Universities', 11th Forum of the European Association for Institutional Research, Trien, 27–30 August.

PAGE E. and A. MIDWINTER (1981) 'Remoteness, Efficiency, Cost and the Reorganisation of Scottish Local Government', *Public Administration*, vol. 58 (Winter).

PAINTER, J. (1991) 'CCT in Local Government: The Final Round', *Public Administration*, vol. 69 (Summer) pp. 191–210.

PARKINSON, M. (1986) 'Creating Accounting and Financial Ingenuity in Local Government: The Case of Liverpool', *Public Money*, vol. 5, no. 4.

PEACOCK, A. and C. WISEMAN (1961) *The Growth of Public Expenditure in Britain* (London: Allen & Unwin).

PERLMAN, M. and B. LYNCH (1979) 'Forecasting, Control and Inflation', *Centre for Environmental Studies Review*, no. 7.

PIRIE, M. (1985) *Privatisation* (London: ASI).

—— (1988) *Micropolitics: The Creation of Successful Policy* (Aldershot: Wildwood House).

—— (1992) *Blueprint for a Revolution* (London: ASI).

POLLITT, C. (1985) 'Measuring Performance: A New System of the National Health Service', *Policy and Politics*, vol. 13, no. 1, pp. 1–15.

—— (1986) 'Beyond the Managerial Model: the case for broadening performance assessment in Government and the public services', *Financial Accountability and Management*, vol. 12, no. 3.

—— (1993) *Managerialism and the Public Services,* 2nd edn (Oxford: Blackwell).

PUNNETT, M. (1985) 'Two Nations? Regional Partisanship 1868–1983', in D. McCrane (ed.), *Scottish Government Yearbook 1985* (Edinburgh: Unit for the study of Government in Scotland).

RAO, M. (1992) *The Changing Role of Local Housing Authorities* (London: Policy Studies Institute).

REGAN, D. E. and J. D. STEWART (1982) 'An Essay in the Government of Health: The Care for Local Authority Control', *Social Policy and Administration*, vol. 16, no. 1 (Spring) pp. 19–61.

RHODES, R. A. W. (1987a) *Beyond Westminster and Whitehall* (London: Unwin Hyman).

—— (1987b) 'Developing the Public Service Orientation', *Local Government Studies* (May/June) vol. 13, no. 3, pp. 63–75.

—— (1992) 'Management in Local Government – Twenty Years On', in S. Leach (ed.), *Strengthening Local Government in the 1990s* (Harlow: Longman Group).

RICHARDSON, J. and G. JORDAN (1982) *Governing under pressure: The Policy: The Policy Process in a Post-Parliamentary Democracy.* (Oxford: Basil Blackwell).

RIDDELL, P. (1983) *The Thatcher Government* (Oxford: Basil Blackwell).

RIDLEY, N. (1973) 'Observations on Niskanen', in *Bureaucracy: Servant or Master?* (London: IEA).

—— (1988) *The Local Right: Enabling Not Providing* (London: CPS).

ROBERTSON, D. (1990) *Choices for Tenants* (Report) (Edinburgh: Scottish Council for Voluntary Organisations).

ROKKAN, A. and D. UNWIN (1983) *Economy, Territory, Identity: Politics of West European Peripheries* (London: Sage).

ROSE, R. and I. McALLISTER (1988) *Voters Begin to Choose?* (London: Sage).

ROSS, J. (1980) 'Local Government Reform in Scotland: Some Subversive ·Reflections' (University of Strathclyde, Mimeo).

SAVAS, E. S. (1987) *Privatization: The Key to Better Government* (Chatham, NJ: Chatham House).

SCHNEIDER, M. (1986) 'Fragmentation at the Growth of Local Government', *Public Choice*, 8, pp. 255–63.

SCHOLES, T. (1994) 'Preparing for Unitary Authorities', Paper presented to the Institute of Rating, Revenues and Valuation Conference, 21 April.

SCOTTISH CONSERVATIVE UNIONIST ASSOCIATION (1992) Report of the Working Party into the Reform of Local Government (unpublished).

SCOTTISH CONSTITUTIONAL CONVENTION (1990) *Towards Scotland's Parliament* (Edinburgh: Report).

SCOTTISH LOCAL GOVERNMENT INFORMATION· UNIT (1988) *A Scottish Guide to the Local Government Act 1988* (Glasgow: SLGIU).

—— (1990) *Community Care – A Priority for the 1990s* (Glasgow: SLGIU).

SCOTTISH OFFICE (1991a) Information Directorate News Release, 23 April (Edinburgh).

—— (1991b) *The Structure of Local Government in Scotland: The Case for Change* (Edinburgh: Scottish Office).

—— (1992a) *Water and Sewerage in Scotland: Investing in Our Future* (Edinburgh: HMSO).

—— (1992b) *Shaping the New Councils* (Edinburgh: HMSO).

—— (1993a) *Responses to the Consultation Paper 'Investing in our Future* (Edinburgh: HMSO).

—— (1993b) *Scotland and the Union*, Report (Edinburgh: HMSO).

—— (1993c) *Statistical Bulletin 1993* (Edinburgh: Scottish Office).

—— (1994) *Draft Guidelines and Compulsory Competitive Tendering and Local Government Reorganisation in Scotland* (Edinburgh: July)

SCOTTISH OFFICE EDUCATION DEPARTMENT (1988) *Self-Governing Schools – Extending Choice for Scottish Parents*, Report (Edinburgh: Scottish Office).

SHARPE, L. J. (1970) 'Theories and Values of Local Government', *Political Studies*, vol. XVIII (June).

SIMON, H. (1958) *Administrative Behaviour* (London: Macmillan).

SKELCHER, C. (1980) 'From Programme Budgeting to Policy Analysis', *Public Administration*, no. 58 (Summer).

SKILDESKY, R. (1989) *Thatcherism* (Oxford: Basil Blackwell).

SLGIU (1992) 'Compulsory Competitive Tendering: Proposals for Change' (Glasgow: SLGIU).

SOCIAL WORK SERVICES GROUP (1991) Statistical Bulletin no. CMCI/ 1991 (Edinburgh: Scottish Office).

SODD (1992) 'Competitive Tendering for Housing Management in Scotland', A Consultation Paper (Edinburgh: Scottish Development Department).

SOED (1992) *Self Governing Schools – Extending Choice for Scottish Parents*, Report (Edinburgh: Scottish Office).

STEWART, A. (1994) 'Single tier authorities offer unique opportunities', *Municipal Journal*, no. 30, pp. 18–19.

STEWART, J. D. (1971) *Management in Local Government: A Viewpoint* (London: Charles Knight).

—— (1982) 'The Role of Information in Public Accountability', in A. Hopwood and C. Tomkins (eds), *Issues in Public Sector Accounting* (London: Philip Allan).

—— (1993) 'The local government review itself reviewed', Paper prepared for the European Policy Forum (July).

STEWART, J. D. and K. WALSH (1989) *In Search of Quality* (Luton: Local Government Training Board).

—— (1992) 'Change in the Management of Public Services', *Public Administration*, vol. 70 (Winter) pp. 499–518.

STODART, A. (1981) *Report of the Committee of Inquiry into Local Government in Scotland* (Edinburgh: HMSO).

STOKER, G. (1988) *The Politics of Local Government* (Basingstoke: Macmillan).

SZYMANSKI, S. and R. WILKINS (1992) *Cheap Rubbish: CCT and Contracting Out Refuse Collection 1981–1988* (London: LBS).

TONGE, R. (1992) 'Financial Management', in D. Farnham and S. Horton (eds), *Managing the New Public Services* (Basingstoke: Macmillan).

TOUCHE ROSS (1992) 'Structure of Local Government in Scotland: Advice on Financial and Qualitative Appraisal of Options for Change' (Edinburgh: Scottish Office).

TRAVERS, T. (1989) 'The Threat to the Autonomy of Elected Local Government', in C. Crouch and D. Marquand (eds), *The New Centralism: Britain Out of Step in Europe?* (London: Basil Blackwell).

—— (1993) 'Professionalism and Local Government Reform: not so much villains as survivors' (unpublished paper).

TRAVERS, T., G. JONES and J. BURNHAM (1993) *The Impact of Population Size on Local Authority Costs and Effectiveness* (York: Joseph Rowntree Foundation).

WALKER, D. (1983) *Municipal Empire: The Town Halls and their Beneficiaries* (London: Temple Smith).

WHEATLEY (1969) *Report of the Royal Commission on Local Government in Scotland* (Edinburgh: HMSO).

WIDDICOMBE (1986b) *The Conduct of Local Authority Business* (Report) Department of the Environment (London: HMSO).

WILDAVSKY, A. (1964) *The Politics of the Budgetary Process*, 3rd edn (New York: Little, Brown).

WILSON, D. J. (1993) 'Turning Drama into Crises: Perspectives on Contemporary Local Government', *Public Policy and Administration*, pp. 30–45.

WISTOW, G., M. KNAPP, B. HARDY and C. ALLEN (1992) 'From Providing to Enabling: Local Authorities and the Mixed Economy of Social Care', *Public Administration*, vol. 70 (Spring) pp. 25–46.

WRIGHT, W. (1977) 'Public Expenditure in Britain – the Crisis of Control', *Public Administration*, vol. 55 (Summer).

—— (1980) From Planning to Control – PESC in the 1970s', in M. Wright (ed.), *Public Spending Decisions* (London: Allen & Unwin).

YOUNG, K. (1986) 'Attitude to Local Government', in the Widdicombe Report Research vol. 111, The Local Government Election (Cmnd 9800; London: HMSO).

YOUNG, R. G. (1981) 'The Management of Political Innovation – The Strathclyde Experience of New Devices for Policy-Making', *Local Government Studies* (Nov./Dec.) pp. 15–31.

—— (1983) 'Scottish Local Government – What Future? in *The Scottish Government Yearbook 1983* (University of Edinburgh).

Index

accountability 34, 36, 82, 86, 95, 105, 136–41, 146, 147
  central government 2
  local government 2, 13, 15
Accounts Commission 40, 44, 52, 62, 143, 144
Adam Smith Institute 99, 118
administrative costs 88, 89
area education boards 95
auditing 25
  powers 28
Audit Commission 39, 42, 44, 70, 81
autonomy 21, 39, 138, 147

bargaining 22, 115
British Constitution 6
budgets 38, 112
  devolved 76, 113
  diversity 22
business planning 131

Cabinet 2, 3
capital allocations 31, 117
capital expenditure 17, 30, 119
capital investment 144
capping 36–9, 111
caravan sites 17
Caring for People, White Paper 71–3
CCT 9, 25, 27, 28, chapter 4 *passim*, 92, 112, 113, 115, 116, 120, 148
centralisation 14, 17, 22, 110
charging 25, 55, 121, 122
children's reporting service 134
choice 9, 25, 28, 64–78, 80
Chope, Christopher 59
Citizen's Charter 45, 55, 86
citizens 19, 39, 56, 123
cleaning of buildings 60
client–contractor split 63, 130

client groups 37
Committee of Inquiry 17
committee system 125
community care 22, 71, 74, 113
community charge 8, 27, 28, 33, 37, 115, 118
community councils 16, 128
comparative indicators 40
competition 25, 28, chapter 4 *passim*
consensus politics 1, 4, 6, 27, 94, 141
Conservatives chapter 1 *passim*, 18, 23, 24, 27, 32, 33, 86, 109, 110, 133, 137
  philosophy 54
  strategy 9, 24, 32, 39
  strongholds 99, 109, 115
  see also Thatcher Government
constitutional change 6, 17
consultation 22, 115, 139
consumer choice 55, 140
consumerism 128, 129
contract model 107, 108
contracting out 58, 59, 121, 124
control 15, 22, 38, 110, 117, 140
coping strategies 33
corporate planning 128, 131
COSLA 5, 21, 31, 44, 76, 86, 107, 115, 118, 142, 147, 151–2
council house sales 4, 27, 68, 115
council tax 34–6, 117, 139
countryside planning 17
creative accounting 33, 119
cultural activities 135
current expenditure guidelines 32

decentralisation 9, 110, 128
decision-making 3, 22, 31, 41, 53, 111, 115, 125, 127

Department of the Environment   34
Department of Social Security   73,
   74, 84
devolved management   76, 116
devolution   2, 5, 16, 86, 157
Direct Labour Organisations (DLOs)
   60, 61
district councils   87, 92, 132
   boundaries   16
   budgets   88
   conflict with regions   17
   control   9
   services   17
Dumfries and Galloway   66

economies of scale   88, 154
economy   27, 31, 40–3, 50
education   4, 16, 77, 112, 116, 121,
   134, 139, 149
   and community involvement   66
   and parental choice   27
   and Roman Catholic schools   64
effectiveness   14, 40–3, 50
efficiency   2, 3, 9, 15, 18, 27, 31,
   40–3, 50, 56, 78, 83, 129, 132,
   138, 140, 152
electoral competition   93
electoral turnout   92
emergency planning   135
enabling authority   78, 79, 85, 113,
   117, 130, 137, 140
environmental and amenity
   services   16, 132
equality   19
European Union   135
evaluation   25
expenditure   18
   and capping controls   27
   and reorganisation   17
   cuts   30
   formula   9

financial controls   22, 110, 112
Financial Management Initiative   41
financial planning   31
financial reforms   111
fire   12, 16, 121, 134, 150

Forsyth, Michael   58, 116
fragmentation   2
Fraser, Lord   8, 34

Grant Aided Expenditure
   Assessments   37, 107
grant penalties   32
grant reductions   32, 112
grants   18, 22, 27, 31, 32, 36–9
Griffiths Report   70, 71, 117
Gross Domestic Product   32
ground maintenance   81

health   4
Heseltine, Michael   34, 86, 110
Highland Region   31
homelessness   77
House of Commons   59
housing   4, 16, 22, 31, 67–9, 74, 77,
   81, 95, 116, 117, 133
   see also council house sales
Housing Revenue Account   67
Housing Scotland (Act) 1988   68
Housing Support Grant   67

ideology   9, 23, 58, 64, 115
implementing reform   142
incremental change   2, 9
inflation   18, 30
inputs   81
Institute of Housing   117

joint arrangements   12, 15, 106
joint boards   15, 29, 106, 107, 134,
   136
joint committees   107, 108, 134, 150

Keynesian consensus   3
King, Tom   111

Labour   4, 6, 16, 30, 31, 120, 133,
   139
Lang, Ian   8, 9, 34, 86, 105, 138
Layfield   22
Liberals   16, 94, 139
leisure and recreation   17
local democracy   15, 19, 136–41, 146
local discretion   19, 22

local government
  and central government 14, 16,
    20–1, 22, 27, 31
  and political choice 18
  and trade unions 26
  and turbulence 26
  classical model 1, 13–18, 130
  elections 19, 20, 92
  finance 30, 157
  fragmentation 25, 111, 136, 153
  functions 12, 87, 90, 103, 104,
    132, 112
  grants 15, 18, 22, 31, 32
  history 11–13
  professionals 14, 23, 116, 119,
    125–7
  polity 18–23
  powers 5, 13
  reform 1, 2, 10, 21, 28, 95, 110,
    111, 131, 139
  role of 19
  satisfaction with 1, 89, 90, 124,
    141
  structure 86, 87
Local Government Information
  Unit 36
Local Government Management
  Board 130
Local Government Planning and
  Land Act (1980) 60
local sensitivity 15
Lothian Region 31

Mains Report 65
Major, John 8, 140
management by objectives 46
managerial agenda 9
managerialist reforms 4, 76, 78,
  114, 124
manpower 121
marginal spending 33
markets 24, 27, 55, 59, 69, 78, 79,
  81, 110, 113, 123, 129, 141
members 17
monetarism 4, 24
monopoly provision 58, 78
Montgomery Inquiry 17

nationalisation of local politics 19
nationalism 3, 6
nature conservation 17
needs assessment 31, 70
neo-Taylorism 79
New Right 4, 23–9, 55, 56, 57, 59,
  87, 116, 118, 120, 128
Next Step Agencies 76
NHS 4, 70, 71, 79
non-compliance 116
non-domestic rates 38

objectives 40, 81, 110
officers 17
opting out 82
option analysis 117
organisational constraints 80
outputs 81

participation 20
partnership 23
penalties 33
performance 80
  assessment 42, 46
  indicators 40–5, 112
  measurement 40, 82, 121
  monitoring 112
  review 40, 42, 46–7
planning 13, 16, 135
planning, programming, budgetary
  systems 40, 46, 51
pluralism 13, 20, 21
police 12, 16, 112, 121, 134, 150
policy choice 114, 126
policy impact 26
political objectives 115
political right 3
poll tax 4, 7, 33–4, 39, 116, 124, 139,
  140
  see also community charge
privatisation 3, 4, 26, 55, 57, 78–85,
  91, 139, 143, 145
public choice 4, 24, 54–8, 123
Public Expenditure Survey 30
public policy 20, 28
public spending 23, 30, 69, 70, 110
purchaser–provider split 75

quality   84, 112, 144
quangos   29
quasi-market models   79, 80, 113

rate capping   32, 37
rates   37
rates revaluation   32
refuse collection   60
regional councils   14, 16, 87, 92, 103,
    132, 149
  abolition   139
  administrative costs   88
  boundaries   16
  conflict with districts   17
  control   9
remoteness   18
reorganisation   14, 86, 93, 95, 110,
    133, 147, 148, 156
representation   19, 125
residential care   69
resource allocation   115
responsibility   82
responsiveness   2, 20, 25
results   82
revenue expenditure   17, 30, 119
Revenue Support Grant   32
Ridley, Nicholas   110, 116
Rifkind, Malcolm   86
roads and transportation   16, 135
role of the state   3, 4, 5, 23, 110

savings   2
school boards   65, 91, 128
School Boards (Scotland) Act
    1988   65
school catering   60
Scottish Constitutional
    Convention   5, 6
Scottish Local Government
    Information Unit (SLGIU)   75
Scottish National Party   16, 94,
    139
Scottish Office   2, 3, 8, 14, 21, 28,
    31, 34, 75, 87, 97, 114, 115
Scottish Office Environment
    Department   117

Scottish Parliament   5–6, 7, 17, 94,
    139
Secretary of State for Scotland   31,
    146
service committees   23
service duplication   89
service levels   19
sewerage   12, 16, 135, 142–7, 150
single-tier authorities   chapter 6
    passim, 118
  costs   152–6
  transferring services   147–52
social work   4, 13, 16, 69–73, 81,
    112, 116, 121, 134, 139, 149
spending   3, 4, 21, 39
Staff Commission   119, 148, 149
Standard Spending Assessments   107
Stodart Report   17, 89, 92
strategic choice   92
strategic services   16
Strathclyde Region   65, 66, 106, 140
street cleansing   60

taxation   19, 21, 23, 30, 110
tenants   77
tenants' association   128
Tenants' Rights, etc. (Scotland) Act
    1980   67
Thatcher Government   3, 4, 30, 116
Thatcher, Margaret   34
Thatcherism   chapter 1 *passim*,
    23–8, 29, 33, 110, 111, 115, 124,
    140
trading accounts   60, 61
trading standards   135
tourism   17
TUPE   148, 151, 152

ultra vires   19
Union, the   2–3, 7, 8, 86
UNISON   151
user charges   27, 57, 121, 122

valuation   136
value for money   15, 29, 39–53, 56,
    88
vehicle repair maintenance   60

virement 31
voting patterns 3, 20, 33
voucher systems 27, 55

war memorials 17
water 12, 16, 135, 139, 142–7, 150
welfare state 4, 9, 13, 70, 124, 141
Welsh Office 34

Western Isles 31
Wheatley 12, 14, 15, 16, 22, 86–8,
    90, 92, 102, 132–6
Whitehall 15
Whitelaw, Willie 116
Widdicombe Committee 13, 20, 89
Working Party on Local Government
    Finance 31, 44, 73